Prophets, Prophecy, and Oracles in the Roman Empire

This book surveys the uses and function of prophecy, prophets, and oracles among Jews, Christians, and pagans in the first three centuries of the Roman Empire and explores how prophecy and prophetic texts functioned as a common language that enabled religious discourse to develop between these groups. It shows that each of these cultures believed that it was in prophetic texts and prophetic utterances that they could find the surest proof of their religious beliefs and a strong confirmation of their group identity.

Leslie Kelly is Associate Professor of History in the School of Arts & Humanities at American Public University, USA.

Routledge Focus on Classical Studies

This new series, part of the Routledge Focus short-form programme, provides a venue for the most up-to-date research in the field of Classical Studies. The series covers a range of topics, from focussed studies on specific texts, figures, or themes, to works on wider issues.

For more information on the Routledge Focus programme, please visit our author information page: www.routledge.com/resources/authors/how-to-publish-with-us

Prophets, Prophecy, and Oracles in the Roman Empire

Jewish, Christian, and Greco-Roman Cultures

Leslie Kelly

LONDON AND NEW YORK

First published 2018
by Routledge

2 Park Square, Milton Park, Abingdon, Oxfordshire OX14 4RN
52 Vanderbilt Avenue, New York, NY 10017

Routledge is an imprint of the Taylor & Francis Group, an informa business

First issued in paperback 2020

Copyright © 2018 Leslie Kelly

The right of Leslie Kelly to be identified as author of this work has been asserted by her in accordance with sections 77 and 78 of the Copyright, Designs and Patents Act 1988.

All rights reserved. No part of this book may be reprinted or reproduced or utilised in any form or by any electronic, mechanical, or other means, now known or hereafter invented, including photocopying and recording, or in any information storage or retrieval system, without permission in writing from the publishers.

Notice:
Product or corporate names may be trademarks or registered trademarks, and are used only for identification and explanation without intent to infringe.

British Library Cataloguing-in-Publication Data
A catalogue record for this book is available from the British Library

Library of Congress Cataloging-in-Publication Data
A catalog record for this book has been requested

ISBN: 978-0-8153-7343-8 (hbk)
ISBN: 978-0-367-60728-9 (pbk)

Typeset in Times New Roman
by Apex CoVantage, LLC

Contents

Introduction

> [T]his people, if they had no means of attaining a knowledge of futurity, being led by the passion common to humanity of ascertaining the future, would have despised their own prophets, as not having in them any particle of divinity; and would not have accepted any prophet after Moses, nor committed their words to writing, but would have spontaneously betaken themselves to the divining usages of the heathen . . . I think, then, that it has been pretty well established . . . that . . . there were prophets among the Jews who uttered not merely general predictions about the future, – as, e.g., regarding Christ and the kingdoms of the world, and the events that were to happen to Israel, and those nations which were to believe on the Saviour, and many other things concerning Him, – but also prophecies respecting particular events.
>
> (Origen, *Against Celsus* 1.36–37)[1]

This statement was made by Origen, an early Christian author, who was arguing against a pagan antagonist, Celsus, in support of Jewish, and ultimately Christian, prophecy (and in particular for his own interpretation of the true meaning of Jewish prophetical writings). According to this passage, it is human, and natural, to practice divination! Divination was omnipresent in the Roman Empire, and it encompassed a wide range of activities. It could include asking the god(s) about the future: one's own future, the future of one's city state, or the future of the Empire. But it could also be an attempt to discern the relationship between the deity (or deities) and humans. Was the relationship good, or did the god(s) require something? Did people need to revive an old rite, establish a new cult, abjure their sins? This book will examine the role that divination played in the first three centuries of the Roman Empire, concentrating on the role of prophets, prophecy, and oracles for the Jewish, Christian, and Greco-Roman cultures. These particular cultures were selected because they provide the fullest extant evidence base and because they have long been the subject of scholarly attention. This allows us to readily identify broad trends in the uses of prophecy and oracles for each group. These three cultures are also a natural choice for comparison because divination formed a part of the religious and political relationships between them.[2] For each culture, there will be a brief survey of each group, with a concentration on the period of heightened activity. In Chapter 1, we will survey trends in Jewish uses of prophets, prophecy, and oracular literature, finishing with a focus on first-century Judaism and the prophets of the first Jewish war against Rome; in Chapter 2, we will survey early Christian engagement with these same forms of divination (prophets, prophecy, and oracles), focusing on second-century "attack-literature"; and in Chapter 3, we will look at divination in pagan Greco-Roman culture, particularly at the flourishing of Neoplatonic interest in oracles and divination in the third century, and the role that oracles played in the Great Persecution in the early fourth century. As we will see, the three groups continually used prophets and prophecy as means of defining themselves and of engaging with each other, in both positive and negative ways.

This study is intentionally text-oriented. It is the literary texts from antiquity that provide us with the best evidence for attitudes toward prophets, prophecy, and oracles. Religious and philosophical works from Plato onward often took up these topics, and in the time of the Roman Empire interest in them was quite high. As will become obvious throughout this study, divination formed part of the repertoire of learned discourse in the Empire about the cosmos and humanity's place within it.

The textual evidence also allows us to draw limited conclusions about the social role of prophets, prophecy, and oracles in the Empire. A good example of this is the dueling oracles in the lead-up to the Diocletianic persecution which was mentioned earlier. To do a full analysis of the social role of divination in the Roman Empire, however, would take a much longer work. Recent scholarship has examined the social function of oracles with respect to risk or uncertainty, or to human intuition.[3] There are also subtopics within the larger category of discourse on prophecy and oracles that this study purposefully eschews. Jews, Christians, Greeks, and Romans all wrote about divination through dreams, the relationship of fate to divination, and the mechanics of divining – how the process worked. To us today, the differences of opinion on these points can be difficult to tease out; they strike one as being overly subtle, not to say tedious. Yet the differences in beliefs on each of these points could indeed have larger implications for the worldview or the faith tradition of groups, not just implications for the individual intellectuals writing about them; and these differences of belief could have real-world consequences.

A good example of this is the way that differences of opinion over the degree of rationality retained by the human medium while in an inspired state impacted the evaluation of Montanists in early Christian orthodox circles.[4] Nevertheless, as whole, these topics take us into the realm of highly technical, narrowly focused discourse, and it is possible to analyze some of the big picture implications of prophets, prophecy, and oracles within and between Judeo-Christian and Greco-Roman cultures, without taking up these topics. Prophets, prophecy, and oracles were operating as a common language in religious and philosophical discourse of the Roman Empire, and we can see this best in the texts of that period that "talk" to each other.

Finally, before turning to our survey, let us briefly define terms. Because there were many ways to divine the future or to try and discover the will of the gods, there are various Greek and Latin terms for divination. The persons who performed divination also had various names. In this work, we will concentrate on the types of divination that were most common to all three cultures that we will be looking at. Briefly, the Greek terms for prophet were *mantis, chrēsmologos*, or *prophētēs*; the Latin, *haruspex, augur, ariolus, vates*.[5] The vocabulary of oracles is similarly diverse. The Latin term for oracle is *oraculum*, from the verb *orare*, to speak. The Greek noun *to manteîon* refers to the seat of an oracle, the oracular center, or it may refer to the response that the oracle provides. Other nouns for the oracular response include *chrēsmos* and *logion*. And there are others.[6] Some of the sources considered are in other languages, such as Aramaic or Coptic. But for our purposes, it will not be important to distinguish between these terms. The vocabulary appears to be used interchangeably in all three cultures.[7]

Notes

1 Unless otherwise noted, all translations in this work are taken from the Ante-Nicene Fathers series or Nicene and Post-Nicene series (for early Christian texts) or the Loeb series (for Jewish, Roman, and Greek texts). All biblical passages are taken from the New Revised Standard Version.

2 Egyptian divination and its relationship to the Roman state and to early Christian communities has been analyzed by Frankfurter, Collins, and Potter, and will be touched upon in Chapter 3, though for reasons of space it was not taken up in this short book.

3 Kim Beerden, *Worlds Full of Signs*: *Ancient Greek Divination in Context* (Leiden; Boston, MA: Brill, 2013), 195–222; Esther Eidinow, *Oracles, Curses, and Risk among the Ancient Greeks* (Oxford: Oxford University Press, 2007); Peter T.

Struck, *Divination and Human Nature: A Cognitive History of Intuition in Antiquity* (Princeton, NJ: Princeton University Press, 2016).

4 See Laura Nasrallah, *An Ecstasy of Folly: Prophecy and Authority in Early Christianity* (Cambridge, MA: Harvard University Press, 2004).

5 David S. Potter, *Prophets and Emperors: Human and Divine Authority from Augustus to Theodosius* (Cambridge, MA: Harvard University Press, 1994), 11; see also Michael Attyah Flower, *The Seer in Ancient Greece* (Berkeley: University of California Press, 2008), 22–23; on the vocabulary of types of possession or inspiration see Nasrallah, *Ecstasy of Folly*, 143.

6 Discussed by Crystal Addey, *Divination and Theurgy in Neoplatonism: Oracles of the Gods* (Burlington, VT: Ashgate, 2014), 6–7.

7 Though it should be noted that J.L. Lightfoot, *The Sibylline Oracles: With Introduction, Translation, and Commentary on the First and Second Books* (Oxford: Oxford University Press, 2007), 20–21, suggests that the Septuagint (the second-century BCE Greek translation of the Jewish Scriptures) and the New Testament do show a tendency to use *prophētēs* rather than *mantis* and its verb form, which were associated with false prophecy rather than true inspiration.

Translations

Fathers of the Third Century: Tertullian, Part Fourth; Minucius Felix; Commodian; Origen, Part First and Second. Translated by Frederick Crombie. Edited by Alexander Roberts and James Donaldson. Revised and chronologically arranged with brief prefaces and occasional notes by A. Cleveland Coxe. Ante-Nicene Fathers 4. New York: Christian Literature Publishing Co., 1885.

Bibliography

Addey, Crystal. *Divination and Theurgy in Neoplatonism: Oracles of the Gods*. Burlington, VT: Ashgate, 2014.

Beerden, Kim. *Worlds Full of Signs: Ancient Greek Divination in Context.* Leiden; Boston, MA: Brill, 2013.

Eidinow, Esther. *Oracles, Curses, and Risk among the Ancient Greeks*. Oxford: Oxford University Press, 2007.

Flower, Michael Attyah. *The Seer in Ancient Greece*. Berkeley: University of California Press, 2008.

Lightfoot, J.L. *The Sibylline Oracles: With Introduction, Translation, and Commentary on the First and Second Books*. Oxford: Oxford University Press, 2007.

Nasrallah, Laura. *An Ecstasy of Folly: Prophecy and Authority in Early Christianity.* Cambridge, MA: Harvard University Press, 2004.

Potter, David S. *Prophets and Emperors: Human and Divine Authority from Augustus to Theodosius*. Cambridge, MA: Harvard University Press, 1994.

Struck, Peter T. *Divination and Human Nature: A Cognitive History of Intuition in Antiquity*. Princeton, NJ: Princeton University Press, 2016.

1 Jewish prophets and prophecy

First-century sectarians, visionaries, and rebels

When referring to Judaism in the Roman Empire, it is commonplace to distinguish between Judaism as it existed before the revolt against the Roman state in the first century CE, which is designated "Second Temple Judaism," and the "Rabbinic Judaism" that existed after this period. The first Jewish revolt occurred in 66–73 CE. At the end of this war, the Temple, around which a large portion of Jewish practice had revolved for centuries, was no more and Jews were forced to pay a special tax. A smaller-scale rebellion broke out in 115–117 CE in Cyprus, Cyrenaica, and Egypt. This was followed by a larger full-scale war, the Bar Kokhba Revolt, 132–136 CE. After this war ended, Jews were forbidden to live in Jerusalem, which was renamed Aelia Capitolina.

The loss of the Temple and Jerusalem necessitated a new form of the faith. In early Israel, the Temple, first begun under King Solomon and completed under David, had been the locus of Yahweh worship. This was destroyed in 587 BCE by Nebuchadnezzar II of Babylonia. After a period in exile in Babylonia, after Cyrus the Great had defeated the Babylonians, Jews returned to Judaea and a second temple was built and temple cult resumed. How much this cult resembled the pre-Babylonian Israelite religion is difficult to decide. In any case, the Temple was once again central from this point up to the destruction in 70 CE. For this reason, this period of time is designated Second Temple Judaism.

There were Jews living outside of Judaea in the Hellenistic and Roman imperial era. Some Jews did not return from Babylon. Egypt also had a large Jewish population from an early period. Jewish mercenaries were serving the Egyptian crown by the fifth century BCE in Elephantine, guarding the border between Egypt and Nubia. They built themselves a local temple. A particularly impactful event that led to a splintering within Judaism was the conflict between the Seleucid ruler of Judaea, Antiochus IV Epiphanes (approximately 215 BCE–164 BCE) and conservative, traditional Jews, living in Jerusalem. Our sources for the Maccabean Revolt are few, and certainly biased, but it appears that internal and external pressure to "Hellenize" as well as desire for political autonomy led to an outbreak of hostilities between the Jews and their Seleucid rulers. In the shifting political and religious alliances of that period, Onias IV, of the line of high priests, left Judaea and created a Jewish community with its own temple at Leontopolis in Egypt. It is also possible, though not certain, that the Jewish community at Qumran, the owners of the texts known today as the Dead Sea Scrolls, broke with the community in Jerusalem at that time.

Jews living outside of Judaea are called "Diaspora Jews" (diaspora meaning "dispersion"). Jews living in the Diaspora sent money to maintain the Temple in Jerusalem, and some may have traveled there for particularly significant festivals, but this would have been impractical for most. Egyptian temples aside, the faith of most Diaspora Jews, as we can see from their extant writings, was not Temple-centered. At some point, the synagogue, a meeting place set aside for communal worship, developed. The earliest archaeological evidence for synagogues has been found outside of Palestine (though they certainly existed there as well). Jewish writings of the Hellenistic Diaspora indicate that Jews were very open to influences from surrounding cultures. Diaspora authors produced such works as drama (influenced by Greek culture), and prose narratives about biblical figures (influenced by Greek romances), which we today call "parabiblical" literature. Philo, a prolific Jewish author from Alexandria in the first century BCE, wrote about the Jewish religion in philosophical terms; Josephus, a Jewish officer in the First Revolt, produced an apology (that is, a defense and explanation, of the Jewish faith) and a history of the Jewish people and a history of the Jewish war. Historical writing had been produced by Jews living in the Hellenistic period, but it survives today only in fragmentary form. The Hellenistic period also produced wisdom literature and apocalypses (influenced by Persian religion), and finally, oracles (influenced by Greek and Ancient Near Eastern paradigms).

We will take up apocalypses below. Two oracles that were composed by Hellenistic Jews were the *Orphica* and the *Sibylline Oracles*. In both cases, a pre-existing Greek oracular tradition was appropriated by a Jewish author to create a pagan oracle interlaced with Jewish themes. According to the early Church historian, Eusebius, the *Orphica* was a second-century BCE work by the Jewish theologian Aristobulus. The narrator is the legendary Greek seer Orpheus, who writes to his son, also a legendary, superhuman seer, Musaeus. The content is monotheistic and it alludes in a veiled way to the Jewish Scriptures. Lines 25–29 of the work refer to a man from long ago, of the race of the Chaldeans, who is granted the ability in spirit to travel through air and water and who was unique. This must refer to either Moses, perhaps the most celebrated Jewish prophet in the Second Temple Period, or Abraham, since there was a tradition that he knew and taught astrology (Eusebius, *Preparation for the Gospel* 9.17.3 and 9.18.2; Josephus, *Antiquities of the Jews* 1.154, 158).

Oracular texts associated with the Sibyls of ancient Greece appeared in Jewish, Christian, and Greco-Roman cultures. The Sibyls were legendary female seers of the Greek world. By the time of the Empire, there were at least ten canonical "Sibyls." Varro, the Augustan-era antiquarian provides a list. The Greek travel writer Pausanias (who lived approximately 110–180 CE) in Book 10 of his *Description of Greece* surveys the legends of the various Sibyls. Oracles associated with them floated around the classical world. The pagan versions of these oracles preserved in literary texts such as Pausanias' indicate that the oracles dealt with such topics as wars, politics, and natural disasters.[1] In 10.12.9 Pausanias notes that one of them was thought by some to have been a Hebrew. A Hellenistic Jewish author adapted these pre-existing oracles. They were then later assembled into twelve books by a Byzantine scholar in the sixth century. We have today Books 1–8, with large portions of Book 7 missing; Books 9–10 are lost; then Books 11–14. Books 1 and 2 go together, and Books 11–14 form a set as well, but these books were not composed all at once. Book 3 may be from a much longer work.[2] Scholars are divided on the provenance and dating of these texts. Later, Christian authors would appropriate the collection and add Christian themes.[3] The Sibylline literature in different forms was still circulated in the Middle Ages. Many scholars think we can get some idea of what the original Jewish layer looked like in Books 1–2 and 3 which have decidedly Jewish material (with occasional Christian interpolations).[4] The Sibyl who speaks in this text is the daughter-in-law of Noah (1.288–90; 3.809–27). It is the Hebrews who will rule (2.174–86). There is a eulogy of the Jewish people in 3.218–64; 3.573–600. Other additions to the oracles include moral exhortations (1.56–148), and apocalyptic scenarios and scenes of cosmic judgment (2.2124–338).[5]

We also see in these Jewish Sibyllines a mixing of the origin stories of pagans and Jews: Noah and the generation after the Flood (1.125–282) appear, but also the Titans (1.307–23). In the oracles, the pagan and Jewish chronologies are combined into one timeline to create the sense of a shared past.[6]

In the case of both of these Jewish oracular compositions, the *Orphica* and the *Sibylline Oracles*, there may be an apologetic function. By appropriating an established, authoritative, pagan voice and having her affirm the Jewish faith, the author seeks to legitimize his religion to his pagan neighbors. This is a pattern that we will see repeated throughout the period of Empire.

Jews of the Roman Empire often interacted with prophecy through texts. They read in the first three centuries old prophecies, including the *Sibylline Oracles*, but also the prophetic passages from their emerging canon of Scripture or holy texts. This consisted of many books of the prophets from Israel's past. There were eventually twenty-four books in the Jewish Scriptures. These were divided into three parts: Torah (that is, "the Teaching," the Five Books of Moses), Nevi'im ("Prophets"), and Ketuvim ("Writings"). It is not known exactly when this canon of books was closed. Josephus provides evidence of twenty-two books marked out in some way by the first century CE (*Against Apion* 1.8).

It is from these that we can reconstruct the paradigm of the prophet in Jewish tradition that would, presumably, have influenced the way that prophets and prophecy was perceived and how it functioned in the Roman Empire. The prophets of Israel were commissioned by God himself (Jeremiah 1:4–5). They did not work for the state. They were tasked with bringing messages from God to the people. Most often these were cautionary messages, exhortations to the people to shape up, and a warning of what the consequences would be if they did not (Ezekiel 33:11). They received visions of the future of Israel and of the heavens. They sometimes engaged in symbolic public acts like the marriage of the prophet Hosea to a whore (symbolizing the relationship between God and Israel). We should note that the Prophets included what we might call histories or chronicles (the Books of Joshua, Judges, Samuel, and Kings) and that Moses and David were also considered prophets by Second Temple Jews and the early Christians. These were men who, according to the Jewish Scriptures, had received special revelations from God.

The word that gets translated as "divination" is in the Jewish Scriptures differentiated from Israelite prophecy. We can see this reflected in the quote from Origen that headed the introduction of this book. The Jewish Scriptures contain injunctions against practicing divination.

> When you come into the land that the Lord your God is giving you, you must not learn to imitate the abhorrent practices of those nations. No one shall be found among you who makes a son or daughter pass through fire, or who practices divination, or is a soothsayer, or an augur, or a sorcerer, or one who casts spells, or who consults ghosts or spirits, or who seeks oracles from the dead. For whoever does these things is abhorrent to the Lord.
>
> (Deuteronomy 18:9–12)

This seems to be one of the ways that Jews were to set themselves apart as a special, holy people. Since they had a special relationship with God, they did not need these other mediums of access. God would tell them what they needed to know without prompting.

Injunctions against divination in some form or other occur in all three of the cultures we will study. This did not mean that these rules were obeyed. There is evidence for Jewish use of amulets, spells, and divination (and also Christian use), but the evidence is for Late Antiquity – post-third century, for the most part.[7] Bohak writes that there is a lack of evidence for divination in the Second Temple period.[8] There is, however, some. The *Treatise of Shem* (first century BCE) is one example.[9] The work characterizes each year according to the sign of the zodiac under which it began. Astrology is attributed to an early, primeval figure, Shem, the son of Noah. Earlier we noted Jewish sources which attributed it to Abraham. Among the writings found at Qumran, there were horoscopes or astrological physiognomies dating to the end of the first century BCE. In one of these texts, the stars at the time of one's birth are paired with one's physical features and so with one's destiny. There is also a record of the interpretation of various prodigies or ill-omens related to the sound of thunder on certain specified days of the month.

> [If in Taurus] it thunders . . . [and] hard labour for the country and sword [in the cour]t of the king and in the country of . . . to the Arabs (?) [. . .] starvation and they will pillage one anoth[er. . .]. [there is a lacuna here] If in Gemini it thunders, terror and affliction (will be brought) by strangers and by. . . .
>
> (column 8, 4Q318)[10]

We will address briefly the presence of the themes of prophets, prophecy, and oracles in Late Antique Jewish texts below.

Apocalyptic writings first appear in Judaism in the Hellenistic era. These are works that describe a vision or revelation given to an individual who appears in the Jewish Scriptures.[11] The visions included typically a review of the past of Israel, its current state of woe, and a warning that a time of even greater conflict was coming, when the righteous and the wicked would have a final battle. The ultimate vindication of the righteous is a consistent theme. Other Second Temple texts may include a vision or prophecy of the future, though in such cases it does not comprise the central focus of the work. We will examine examples of these types of texts below.

In order to fully understand the social and religious role that these texts played, we must know who was reading them. Catherine Hezser, in a major study, *Jewish Literacy in Roman Palestine* (2001), concludes that literacy among Jews in Roman imperial Palestine was relatively low. Hezser, surveying the evidence for education and use of texts in synagogues, concludes that in comparison to Roman society, we see far less use of writing among Jews in Palestine.[12] She also notes the use of a reader in the synagogues.[13] Even if Jewish persons were having the Scriptures regularly read to them, we still do not know who was reading the apocalypses, the parabiblical narratives, or the oracles, or how much exposure they had to them. There is a range of indications in the texts themselves which do not allow us to draw firm conclusions. In the *Testament of Moses*, for example, Moses advises Joshua how to care for the writings he will leave behind. Joshua is to preserve them carefully in a specially designated place "until the day of recompense when the Lord will surely have regard for his people" (1.17–18).[14] In *4 Ezra* 12.38 Ezra is commanded to write these things down and hide the text. Some of the teachings are to be public, some are for the wise only (14.26; these are divided into twenty-four public books and seventy secret ones in 14.47–48). In *2 Baruch*, Baruch is commissioned to write a letter to share the message from God with the people living in Babylon (code for "Diaspora"; 77.14), and they are instructed to read it regularly in the assemblies (86.1).

Beginning in the first century CE, Christian communities would begin to appropriate some of these Jewish texts, adding to them and producing their own apocalypses and parabiblical narratives. These non-canonical writings are barely mentioned in the rabbinic literature of Late Antiquity. We cannot say for certain, however, that these texts were simply conceded to the Christians since visionary parabiblical literature was produced in the medieval era, some of it closely related to the Second Temple texts.[15] This implies continuity.

In one case, we do know who was reading what. This is the community at Qumran. The Qumran site is located on the Dead Sea, near Jordan. The Jews living at Qumran were a sectarian group who had splintered off from the religious establishment in Jerusalem. They considered themselves to be the true Israel and expected the nations and the Jewish community to fall subject to divine punishment for impiety. During the first Jewish war against Rome, they fled, hiding their collection of scrolls in caves. Though some of the writings from the Dead Sea that we will discuss below predate our chosen period of focus, the indications are that these texts were still being read by the community at Qumran in the first century CE. There is a wide range of materials in the collection. One important text that gives us a window into their approach to prophecy is the *Commentary on Habakkuk* (1QpHab). This text dates to 31–30 BCE. Column 1 of *Habakkuk* begins with the first line of the biblical book: "[*Oracle of Habakkuk the prophet. How long, O Lord, shall I cry*] *for help and Thou wilt not* [*hear*]?" This is followed by interpretation: "[Interpreted, this concerns the beginning] of the [final] generation." The second column gives us important information about the way that prophecies of the Jewish Scriptures were interpreted in the community and who was the authorized interpreter.

> [*Behold the nations and see, marvel and be astonished; for I accomplish a deed in your days, but you will not believe it when*] **II** *told* [Habakkuk 1:5]. [Interpreted, this concerns] those who were unfaithful together with the Liar, in that they [did] not [listen to the word received by] the Teacher of Righteousness from the mouth of God. And it concerns the unfaithful of the New [Covenant] in that they have not believed in the Covenant of God [and have profaned] His holy Name. And likewise, this saying is to be interpreted [as concerning those who] will be unfaithful at the end of days. They, the men of violence and the breakers of the Covenant, will not believe when they hear all that [is to happen to] the final generation from the Priest [in whose heart] God set [understanding] that he might interpret all the words of His servants the Prophets, through whom He foretold all that would happen to His people and [His land].

Other passages refer to the Kittim (that is, foreigners) and the destruction they bring, and to the Teacher of Righteousness (column 7), who is able to interpret "all the mysteries of the words of His servants the Prophets." Column 9 refers to a Wicked Priest who was punished by God for his betrayal of the Teacher of Righteousness. The community interprets the prophetical writings of the Jewish Scriptures in light of their present situation. Habakkuk was writing about them! And this correct interpretation of these prophetic texts is possible because they have an inspired interpreter. The prophetical writings have to be carefully interpreted – there is much potential to get it wrong – but wise persons, the leaders of their own community, specifically the Teacher of Righteousness, are divinely enabled to do it.[16]

Other sectarian texts (that is texts at Qumran that are directed inwardly at this specific community and include rules of the community or an explication of its unique history and future) exhibit a similar approach. Another strong example is the first-century BCE–first-century CE text, *The War Scroll*. Inspired by the Book of Daniel, it describes a final battle against the Kittim, or foreigners, who in this case are clearly the Romans. It draws on prophetic books of the Jewish Scriptures and contains new prophecies: the righteous army will fight the Kittim and will experience terrible tribulation but will ultimately prevail and enter into "eternal redemption" (column 1). The formations and preparations of the troops are laid out in detail, as well as the directions as to how the troops will praise the Lord for the victory. In the closely related *Book of War*, the biblical prophetic books of Ezekiel and Isaiah are interpreted with reference to this period, and the Branch of David will be instrumental in defeating the foe (4Q285, fr. 7; see also the *Community Rule* and the *Damascus Document*).

In addition to these sectarian writings and to several commentaries on books of the prophets from the Jewish Scriptures, there are fragments of parabiblical writings associated with the prophets of the Jewish Scriptures. *Pseudo-Ezekiel*[a–d] dates to the mid-first century BCE and is modeled on the biblical book of Ezekiel. It includes Ezekiel's vision of the chariot of God (which is found in the biblical text); God commands Ezekiel to prophesy regarding the destruction of the nations. Josephus (*Jewish Antiquities* 10.5.1) records that Ezekiel had written two books predicting the Babylonian defeat of Jerusalem, destruction of the first Temple, and enslavement of the Jewish people in Babylon as well as the second destruction of the people and fall of the Temple in Josephus' own day at the hands of the Romans. There appears to have been a number of parabiblical traditions circulating about Ezekiel in both the rabbinic Jewish and early Christian communities.[17] At Qumran there were also parabiblical writings about the prophets Jeremiah, Elisha, Daniel, and Moses (which last, 4Q375, includes how to test prophets). Apocalyptic visionary texts from Qumran include the *Apocalyptic Chronology* or *Apocryphal Weeks* (4Q247), the *Aramaic Apocalypse* and *Jubilees*, a second-century BCE text, which records God's revelation to Moses about the future of Israel and the way they are to conduct themselves. It attributes the origins of astrological knowledge to the Watchers or fallen angels who were responsible for bringing corruption into the word (8.1–4; Cainan discovers their writings).

From this short survey we can deduce that the Qumran community had a strong interest in prophecy and used prophetic texts to shape their own identity. This group exhibits two trends: appropriation of past prophetic texts and production of new prophetical texts. In both cases, prophecies serve to define this community over against the outside world. Their interpretive strategy is a simple one: the righteous (that's them!), though brought low in the present time, will in the future be exalted. Their enemies will be brought to destruction. They should not worry about their present, depressed situation: the fact that they are experiencing hardship and rejection should be understood as proof that the prophecies of the past were real: it was foretold that the righteous would experience a period of suffering; consequently, suffering in the present must equate to future exaltation.

If we look at texts outside of Qumran, aside from the sectarian writings describing community rules and recording a history of conflict with the establishment in Judaea, we find similar visionary texts conveying similar types of messages. The book of *1 Enoch*, for example, is like the book of *Jubilees* discussed in the Qumran section earlier, a work that uses biblical characters who have a vision which delivers to them a special revelation from God, and it has a strong interest in explaining the origin of evil. Book 2 of this composite work dates to the end of the first century BCE or the beginning of the first century CE.[18] In the section *The Book of the Similitudes*, Enoch delivers the message that the wicked shall be judged and the righteous vindicated. He describes his heavenly visions, which include how judgment is carried out and how the cosmos works; he shares how in the final judgment all shall be resurrected and the righteous sifted out. The judgment of the fallen angels (which were referenced in *Jubilees*) is also described (55). These renegade angels were responsible for the evil and corruption in the world. They had come down from heaven to mingle with human women and had taught human beings things that they were not supposed to know – some of which were overtly evil (such as sorcery, 65.6) but some of which were what we might call "neutral" knowledge, such as writing (69.9). Several parabiblical writings from antiquity include some version of this primeval episode; the new knowledge taught by the fallen angels is bad because it resulted in a more complicated, complex world. In *Jubilees*, the knowledge brought to man is divination (8.3; 93–94). Reed, in her book *Fallen Angels*, notes that in that text, divination is strongly related to intermarriage with foreigners and so serves a symbolic purpose (see 8.3).[19] In *1 Enoch*, the fallen angels will be punished by the Flood, and man, too, will be punished. In the earlier section of *1 Enoch*, the *Book of the Watchers* (comprising chapters 1–36 of our present text), the mixing of heavenly beings with human women leads to the creation of a hybrid group of beings, the Watchers, and from them come the evil spirits that corrupted the earth (15).

The next grouping is those texts that respond to the destruction of the Jewish Temple in 70 CE. This message, that destruction is only a temporary punishment, is repeated in other Second Temple prophetic texts that were produced as a response to the fall of the Temple.

The book of *4 Ezra* forms part of *2 Esdras*, a book which is found in the Apocrypha section of English Bibles. It is itself a composite work, which was added to over time and includes in its present form Christian interpolations. The Jewish layer, as we may call it, consists of chapters 3–14. This section of *4 Ezra* dates to the post-70 CE destruction of Jerusalem and the fall of the Temple and is an attempt to understand what happened.[20] The literary setting of the first-century Jewish section is the Babylonian Captivity of the sixth century BCE. Babylon, in this work, as was common for both Jewish and Christian texts, is symbolic in this text. By placing the prophet in this past situation of trauma, the author of the text signals to the reader: the present can be understood by looking to the past. In our text, a prophet Ezra, also called Salathiel, being captive in Babylon, asks the Lord why this terrible calamity has been allowed to befall Israel (3.1–4), and he attempts to comfort the people (12.40–51). He engages in a dialogue with an angel who tells him that the end of days is near (4.1–5.20). The angel reveals the divisions of time and the signs of the coming end of days (6.7–28). The angel explains that the sins of Israel have led to her being punished (7.10–9.25). In 11.1–12.39, Ezra has a dream vision of an eagle, and his angelic interpreter describes how a great kingdom (Rome) will be used as an instrument of punishment, but a Messiah will come and succeed him and preserve a remnant of the holy.

The book of *2 Baruch* (also known as the *Syriac Apocalypse of Baruch*) has a similar background.[21] It is also believed to have been originally composed as a response to the destruction of 70 CE, and like *4 Ezra* the narrator takes on the persona of a biblical prophet, this time Baruch from the biblical book of Jeremiah, the scribe who assisted that prophet. In this case, too, the narrative framework is the fall of Jerusalem under Babylon, and Baruch is commissioned to speak to the people to explain events and to console them. God promises to show Baruch what will happen in the end of days. Like Ezra, Baruch questions the mercy of God, and it is explained to him that Israel has sinned and must be punished. Baruch is given the signs of the end times. He admonishes the people to observe the Law, because in this way only will they be granted salvation (44.1–15; 46.5–7; 51.7–12).

The books of *4 Ezra* and *2 Baruch* come from a similar social milieu and speak to the same historical event. While there are some differences in their approaches, this is more a matter of where the emphasis is placed than any actual disjunct in worldview or in theology.[22] By and large they are in agreement as to the cause of the destruction of Jerusalem and the future of Israel. The people of Israel have sinned (*4 Ezra* 6.17–20; 7.70–74; *2 Baruch* 1.3–4; 15.1–8). They will be chastised by being allowed to suffer at the hands of the Romans (*4 Ezra* 7.10–12; *2 Baruch* 1.5; 5.3; 6.9). The overarching message, however, is one of consolation for the Jewish people. In the end, the Roman nation will be destroyed (*4 Ezra* 12.10–32; *2 Baruch* 39.1–8), and the righteous ones, those people of Israel who have tried to keep the Law, will be granted heavenly salvation (*4 Ezra* 14.33–35; see also *4 Ezra* 8.29–36 and 8.47–52, where Ezra is said to be a part of this group; *2 Baruch* 15.1–8).

In the Jewish texts that we have examined so far, prophecy serves as an important tool, a resource that they can call upon to respond to situations of conflict and trauma. A beleaguered community, with a received tradition of prophetic texts, looks to these writings to help them make sense of their present and to give them hope for the future. This prophetic collection is then added to, and a plethora of prophecies reassures them that their present situation is not a mistake, but rather part of a larger plan that is leading to better things. To us, looking back and reading these texts together, all at once, it seems perhaps superfluous to have so many texts that are more or less providing the same message. But the high production, the compulsion to create more narratives of victory, is likely an indication of the feeling of extreme stress that the Jewish community experienced at this time in history. Jewish authors of the Second Temple period did not only respond to crisis through production and exegesis of prophetic texts. But even other genres, to which we will turn next, did include discussions of prophecy.

The writings of our two most prolific, extant, first-century Jewish intellectual authors, Philo and Josephus, indicate that both men had a strong interest in prophecy.[23] Philo, an Alexandrian Jew with a background in philosophy, expresses an interest in how prophecy works (*Who Is the Heir of Divine Things*?), in true versus false prophecy (Philo, *The Special Laws*), and in famous prophets (Moses in particular, see *On the Life of Moses* 2.187–88, 246, 264–65, 268–69). Philo demonstrates an approach to the prophetic writings of the Jewish Scriptures that is very like that of the Qumran community – that is, he believes in inspired interpretation.

In Philo's writings, the inspired interpreters are Moses and Philo himself. In the *Decalogue*, Philo writes:

> For it was in accordance with His nature that the pronouncements in which the special laws were summed up should be given by Him in His own person, but the particular laws by the mouth of the most perfect of the prophets [Moses] whom He selected for his merits and having filled him with the divine spirit, chose him to be the interpreter of His sacred utterances.
>
> (*Decalogue* 33)

In *On the Migration of Abraham* 7, Philo describes how he himself is able to explicate the Jewish Scriptures because he is guided by a divine inspiration: "I have approached my work empty and suddenly become full, the ideas falling in a shower from above and being sown invisibly" (*On the Migration of Abraham* 7; compare *On Dreams* 1.26 and *On the Cherubim* 27).

Why does Philo engage so fervently with prophetic texts? For him, too, prophecy is proof.

> Then, indeed, we find him [Moses] possessed by the spirit, no longer uttering general truths to the whole nation but prophesying to each tribe in particular the things which were to be and hereafter must come to pass. Some of these have already taken place, others are still looked for, since confidence in the future is assured by fulfilment in the past.
>
> (*On the Life of Moses* 2.51)

We will find a similar sentiment expressed in Josephus and in the early Christian authors. It is also similar to what we have already seen in the Dead Sea community and in the parabiblical texts produced in the wake of the Jewish war: if they can prove to their own satisfaction that some of the prophecies in the texts they consult have been fulfilled, then that gives them reassurance as to what the future will hold. The prophetic passages for the Qumran community indicated a future vindication; for Philo they indicate a loving God, one who is very congenial to him personally, as God is a being of Goodness and Reason.

Josephus, our other first-century Jewish intellectual, also believed in inspired interpretation, and he also looks to the Jewish Scriptures to help him understand his present situation. In the following passage, Josephus describes himself as an inspired interpreter of dreams and of the "sacred books."

> But as Nicanor was urgently pressing his proposals and Josephus overheard the threats of the hostile crowd, suddenly there came back into his mind those nightly dreams, in which God had foretold to him the impending fate of the Jews and the destinies of the Roman sovereigns. He was an interpreter of dreams and skilled in divining the meaning of ambiguous utterances of the Deity; a priest himself and of priestly descent, he was not ignorant of the prophecies in the sacred books. At that hour he was inspired to read their meaning, and, recalling the dreadful images of his recent dreams, he offered up a silent prayer to God. "Since it pleases thee," so it ran, "who didst create the Jewish nation, to break thy work,

> since fortune has wholly passed to the Romans, and since thou hast made choice of my spirit to announce the things that are to come, I willingly surrender to the Romans and consent to live; but I take thee to witness that I go, not as a traitor, but as thy minister."
>
> (*Jewish War* 3.351–54; compare 3.399–408)

So far in our survey of Jewish divination in the Roman Empire, we have been examining early Jewish engagement with prophetic texts. Josephus' description of the Jewish war indicates the prominent role that active, live (!) prophets and prophecy took in this confrontation with Rome. According to Josephus' account, nationalistic leaders stirred up the people of Jerusalem using prophecy. Declaring themselves to be God-sent, these men promised that they would lead the Jewish nation to victory against the Romans. Not all of the men cited below are specifically termed "prophets" by Josephus, but he uses similar language to describe all of these individuals and seems to lump them all together, as in this passage:

> Moreover, impostors and deceivers called upon the mob to follow them into the desert. For they said that they would show them unmistakable marvels and signs that would be wrought in harmony with God's design. Many were, in fact, persuaded and paid the penalty of their folly.
>
> (*Jewish Antiquities* 20.167–68; *Jewish War* 2.259)

A good example of this type of prophetic actor is Theudas. Calling himself a prophet, he led his followers to the River Jordan, declaring that he would part it. This was apparently intended as a prophetic sign, such as the prophets of the Jewish Scriptures had performed, and we see other prophetic pretenders (as Josephus would call them) making similar promises (*Jewish Antiquities* 18.85–86; 20.169–72; *Jewish War* 2.261–63; *Antiquities* 20.188). Theudas was put down by Fadus the procurator; Acts 5:36 gives the number of his followers as being about four hundred (Josephus, *Antiquities of the Jews* 20.97; Eusebius, *Church History* 2.11.1–3).

Josephus believed that the present age, his own times, had been foretold in the Jewish Scriptures. In *Jewish War* 6.300–309, he recounts with approval a prophet who had foretold a coming "woe" to Jerusalem which he repeated for seven years and five months. This country dweller, Jesus, son of Ananias, began his prophecy of doom four years prior to the outbreak of the war. For his pains he was beaten by both the people and the Roman procurator who declared him insane. He was killed during the siege. But Josephus believes he had it right. In *Jewish War* 4.377, Josephus records that the faction known as the Zealots dismissed the notion, which was evidently circulating at the time, that the Jewish Scriptures had foretold the destruction of Jerusalem in the present age. When Josephus was sent by Titus to parley with the Jews still under siege, Josephus appeals to the proof of prophecy to encourage the Jewish forces to surrender. An ancient oracle, he says, has predicted the destruction of the Jews (*Jewish War* 6.109–10).[24] Like the Qumran community, Josephus searches the Scriptures and finds a way to frame the present. He believes that this is the reason prophecies were given by God in the first place:

> Reflecting on these things one will find that God has a care for men, and by all kinds of premonitory signs shows His people the way of salvation, while they owe their destruction to folly and calamities of their own choosing. Thus the Jews, after the demolition of Antonia, reduced the temple to a square, although they had it recorded in their oracles that the city and the sanctuary would be taken when the temple should become four-square. But what more than all else incited them to the war was an ambiguous oracle, likewise found in their sacred scriptures, to the effect that at that time one from their country would become ruler of the world. This they understood to mean someone of their own race, and many of their wise men went astray in their interpretation of it. The oracle, however, in reality signified the sovereignty of Vespasian, who was proclaimed Emperor on Jewish soil. For all that, it is impossible for men to escape their fate, even though they foresee it. Some of these portents, then, the Jews interpreted to please themselves, others they treated with contempt, until the ruin of their country and their own destruction convicted them of their folly.
>
> (*Jewish Wars* 6.310–15)

It is worth noting that Josephus' prophecies concerning the future emperor Vespasian, the fate of the people of Jotapata, and himself, were taken seriously by Vespasian and account for his favorable treatment by the Romans (Josephus, *Jewish War* 3.399–407).

There were other Jewish prophets, active in Palestine and unconnected with the war or politics. John the Baptist, although he does attack Herod, concentrates primarily on moral exhortation (Luke 1:76–79; Matthew 3:1–11; 14:1–11). Acts 16:16 mentions a prophetic slave woman in Philippi whose master rents out her services. Celsus, a second-century pagan opponent of the Christians, had complained of the many prophets still active in Phoenicia and

Palestine (Origen, *Against Celsus* 7.3), though it must be noted that prophets do not appear often in the earliest rabbinic literature. The role seems to have faded out by the end of the second century. And to this list we must add also Jesus of Nazareth, who was perceived as a prophet as least by some pagans (according to *Against Celsus* 2.14, Phlegon of Tralles, in his work, *Chronicles*, had described Jesus as a truthful prophet).

I have chosen to concentrate in this chapter on the first century CE, as it was a high point for Jewish prophetic activity and discourse about prophecy. What happened to the themes of prophecy, prophets, and oracles in Judaism after the first century CE? They did not disappear entirely; another work that reflects on the destruction of the Second Temple, *3 Baruch*, was produced sometime in the second century CE. Themes of *3 Baruch* include cosmological knowledge (how the cosmos works) and the fate of souls after death.[25] This text does not depict a final eschatological vindication of the righteous keepers of the Law. The message of this text is that the way to salvation lies neither in the Law, nor the Temple and the rituals associated with it, but rather in simply right living. This path is open to all. In contrast to *4 Ezra* and *2 Baruch*, *3 Baruch* has a universalist outlook.[26]

If we look for patterns in rabbinic literature from Late Antiquity, we can only say that rabbinic literature does not exhibit one unified view on the possibly of continuing prophecy. Stephen Cook notes that some rabbinic texts reflect the notion that Jewish prophecy ceased after the Persian period, that is, after the prophetical books of Haggai, Zechariah, and Malachi. We can see this in *Tosefta Sotah* 13.3 and so forth.[27] Isaac Gottlieb notes that there are rabbinic passages that suggest that the end of prophecy came with the advent of Alexander the Great or, alternatively, with the fall of the Second Temple (*Seder Olam* 30).[28] There are two passages in rabbinic literature that suggest that prophecy could not take place outside of the land of Israel (Babylonian Talmud, *Mo'ed Katan* 25a).[29] There are also passages that say that at the end of time all Jews will be able to prophesy (*Tanhuma Beha'alotekha* 17), or even that prophecy will become a universal gift for all humankind (*Aggadat Bereshit* 68).[30] In surveying and categorizing the rabbinic literature with respect to usage and evaluation of the prophetical books of the Jewish Scriptures, the conclusions of Isaac Gottlieb and Jacob Neusner complement one another: Neusner demonstrates through numerous illustrating passages that the rabbis did not take each prophet on his own terms; they were rather looking to harmonize the message of each and to make them all fit within their overarching system of law and theology.[31] Gottlieb identifies as consistent themes those of repentance, consolation, and the loving-kindness of God.[32]

In rabbinic literature there is no interest in visions of the end times. Lester Grabbe puts it this way:

> The Yavnean traditions say little or nothing about eschatology. The rabbinic traditions being developed in the wake of the fall of Jerusalem seem to be saying that the answer to the situation of the Jews is that a temple is not needed, and the key to the practice of the Jewish religion is found in study of the Torah and the living of one's daily life according to it.
>
> In such a scenario, eschatology played no role. As a prime example, the view of the messiah in early rabbinic tradition illustrates the situation. At a time when messianic expectations seem to have been widespread within Judaism (i.e., the period between the 66–70 and the Bar Kokhva revolts), the rabbinic traditions show little interest. As time goes on, a modified messianic figure is developed who takes a restricted role in the indefinite future. It is true that periodically within rabbinic Judaism, messianic figures did arise, but these were exceptional; the focus in rabbinic Judaism was different.
>
> Why? The matter is not addressed explicitly and must be inferred. But one explanation is that eschatological speculation was too unreliable or discredited or dangerous. For the sages there was no messiah and no imminent apocalypse; there was only "Moses our rabbi" and the careful study of what he had taught.[33]

However we may explain it, there was no interest in predicting the future but only an interest in explaining tradition. According to Martin Jaffee, the producers of rabbinic literature understood their primary role as that of shapers of a pre-existing tradition: "They are not authors but repeaters (*Tanna'im*) and 'explainers' (*'Amora'im*); they do not invent, they merely transmit."[34]

As we come to the end of this brief survey of Jewish prophecy in the early Roman Empire, we should pause a moment to consider the relationship between texts and reality. Scholars have disagreed over the connection between the literary depictions of Jewish prophets and what they were actually like "on the ground." Horsley cautioned that literary descriptions do not necessarily reflect reality.[35] Grabbe points out that literary depictions of prophets may in fact influence the reality – that the two may be mutually reinforcing.[36]

Let us also go back briefly to the relationship between present status and expressions of woe. Some scholars think that we can best understand the type of prophecy and prophetic texts being produced in first-century CE Judaism as a response to a feeling of dissatisfaction with one's present status. There is a disconnect between the (low) status of the here and now and the (better) past which results in expressions of hope for a glorious future.[37] Other scholars believe that we should understand first-century prophecy and prophetic textual production as the result of an apocalyptic mindset. That is, Jews of this era believed that they were living in the age of the end times, an age when the prophecies of the past that promised a future period of conflict for the righteous followed by a time of vindication was at last upon them, or at least being set in motion.[38]

Although we can identify some texts that address particular situations (the Qumran community and *Habakkuk*; the relationship between *2 Baruch* and the destruction of the Temple), the genre as a whole cannot be reduced to one factor. Apocalyptic works themselves contain many other aspects in addition to images of destruction and vindication, and other types of parabiblical writings incorporate apocalyptic sections into works which clearly have other themes. In the *Testament of Abraham*, for example, a work which in its present form probably dates to the third or fourth century CE, the heavenly visions granted to Abraham serve to reassure the reader that death is nothing to be feared. The soul will be given a secure home with a merciful God; death is not the end and judgement will be lenient. And we have left out much in this brief survey.

One consistent pattern that we can identify is that of appropriation. To engage with prophecy was a common experience for all of the groups discussed in this chapter (pagans, sectarian Jews, zealot Jews, Jews on good terms with the Roman state); all of these persons believed in prophecy – that some human beings could receive accurate messages about the future from the Divine; that the Divine being(s) communicated with human beings through the medium of prophetic persons and through prophetic texts. But it was not always used to unite (as in the production of Jewish *Sibylline Oracles* which demonstrated a shared past between pagans and Jews) but rather was used to attack other groups: to identify them as enemies (as for example the Qumran group who interpreted the religious establishment at Jerusalem as the evil entities mentioned in the Jewish Scriptures and depicted them in that role in their own new prophetic texts) or to denigrate their flawed interpretation of prophetic texts (as for example Josephus' anti-zealot comments). Prophecy in this period of early Roman imperial Judaism is a tool of apology, identity construction, and a means of understanding the past, present, and future.

Notes

1 For a discussion see John J. Collins, *Seers, Sibyls & Sages in Hellenistic-Roman Judaism* (Leiden: E.J. Brill, 1997), 182–84; Matthew Neujahr, *Predicting the Past*

in the Ancient Near East: Mantic Historiography in Ancient Mesopotamia, Judah, and the Mediterranean World (Providence, RI: Brown Judaic Studies, 2012), 195–242.

2 H.W. Parke, *Sibyls and Sibylline Prophecy in Classical Antiquity* (London: Routledge, 1988), 6.

3 For bibliography on the Sibylline Oracles, see James R. Davila, *The Provenance of the Pseudepigrapha: Jewish, Christian, or Other?* (Leiden: Brill, 2005), 180 n. 1 and Neujahr, *Predicting the Past*, chapter 6.

4 Such as passages on the life and Incarnation of Christ as well as anti-Hebrew passages, see for example 1.324–400.

5 Collins, *Seers*, 189–90; Neujahr, *Predicting the Past*, 249–81 argues that the Jewish *Sibylline Oracles* were indebted to Greek oracular verse and incorporated Egyptian themes.

6 J.L. Lightfoot, *The Sibylline Oracles: With Introduction, Translation, and Commentary on the First and Second Books* (Oxford: Oxford University Press, 2007), 23.

7 See Gideon Bohak, *Ancient Jewish Magic* (Cambridge: Cambridge University Press, 2008) and Marvin W. Meyer and Richard Smith, eds., *Ancient Christian Magic: Coptic Texts of Ritual Power* (Princeton, NJ: Princeton University Press, 1999).

8 Bohak, *Ancient Jewish Magic*, notes that the Septuagint "translates the biblical prohibitions against consulting various magicians and diviners . . . into the Greek terms of its own time," 77; see Lester Grabbe, *Judaic Religion in the Second Temple Period: Belief and Practice from the Exile to Yavneh* (London: Routledge, 2000), 233 for relationship between the Hebrew word for prophecy and the Greek term; few texts of this period are in Hebrew.

9 For an introduction, translation, and commentary see J.H. Charlesworth, "*Treatise of Shem* (First Century B.C.): A New Translation and Introduction," in *The Old Testament Pseudepigrapha*: *Volume One*: *Apocalyptic Literature and Testaments*, ed. James H. Charlesworth (1983; repr., Peabody, MA: Hendrickson, 2016), 473–86.

10 All translations and dates for the scrolls are taken from Geza Vermes, *The Complete Dead Sea Scrolls*, 7th rev. ed. (London: Penguin Classics, 2012).

11 Grabbe stresses the many parallels between what we today call prophetic writings and apocalyptic writings. He suggests that apocalyptic is best seen as a sub-genre of prophecy though likely social changes might well have influenced the form of any given prophetic writing and its themes or outlook, Grabbe, *Judaic Religion*, 234–35; contrast Ben Witherington, *Jesus the Seer: The Progress of Prophecy* (Peabody, MA: Hendrickson, 1999), 352.

12 Catherine Hezser, *Jewish Literacy in Roman Palestine* (Tübingen: Mohr Siebeck, 2001), 500; on Roman writing see Elizabeth Meyer, *Legitimacy and Law in the Roman World: Tabulae in Roman Belief and Practice* (New York: Cambridge University Press, 2004).

13 Hezser, *Jewish Literacy*, 454.

14 This translation is taken from that of J. Priest, "*Testament of Moses* (First Century A.D.): A New Translation and Introduction," in *The Old Testament Pseudepigrapha*: *Volume One*: *Apocalyptic Literature and Testaments*, ed. James H. Charlesworth (1983; repr., Peabody, MA: Hendrickson, 2016), 919–34.

15 A good example of this is the *Aramaic Levi* text. This is a first-century BCE text. The *Aramaic Levi* document was used as a source for the *Testament of Levi*, itself part of a larger work, the *Testament of the Twelve Patriarchs*, which was read and preserved by Christians (who sometimes preserved wording, but at other times felt free to adapt it extensively); for an introduction, translation, and commentary see James R. Davila, "*Aramaic Levi*: A New Translation and Introduction," in *Old Testament Pseudepigrapha: More Noncanonical Scriptures: Volume One*, eds. Richard Bauckham, James R. Davila, and Alexander Panayotov (Grand Rapids, MI: William B. Eerdmans, 2013), 121–42.

16 Inspired interpretation in Second Temple Judaism has been discussed by several scholars, including Vermes, *Complete Dead Sea Scrolls*, 70–71; Grabbe, *Judaic Religion*, 238 and Neujahr, *Predicting the Past*, 182–84. This concept will be discussed again below. Some scholars see this approach to Scripture as further proof that this community at Qumran was in fact an Essene community as it aligns with the description of that group in Josephus, *Jewish War* 2.159 (discussed in Neujahr, *Predicting the Past*, 182–84). But the practice seems to be widespread.

17 See Benjamin G. Wright, "*The Apocryphon of Ezekiel*: A New Translation and Introduction," in *Old Testament Pseudepigrapha: More Noncanonical Scriptures: Volume One*, eds. Richard Bauckham, James R. Davila, and Alexander Panayotov (Grand Rapids, MI: William B. Eerdmans, 2013), 380–92, especially 380–86.

18 On *1 Enoch*, see especially Annette Yoshiko Reed, *Fallen Angels and the History of Judaism and Christianity: The Reception of Enochic Literature* (Cambridge: Cambridge University Press, 2006).

19 Ibid., 92–94.

20 For an introduction, translation, and commentary see B.M. Metzger, "*The Fourth Book of Ezra* (Late First Century A.D.) with the Four Additional Chapters: A New Translation and Introduction," in *The Old Testament Pseudepigrapha: Volume One: Apocalyptic Literature and Testaments*, ed. James H. Charlesworth (1983; repr., Peabody, MA: Hendrickson, 2016), 517–59.

21 For an introduction, translation, and commentary see A.F.J. Klijn, "*2 (Syriac Apocalypse of) Baruch* (Early Second Century A.D.): A New Translation and Introduction," in *The Old Testament Pseudepigrapha: Volume One: Apocalyptic Literature and Testaments*, ed. James H. Charlesworth (1983; repr., Peabody, MA: Hendrickson, 2016), 615–52.

22 The book of *4 Ezra* has more emphasis on the inscrutable ways, as Daschke (145) puts it, of God (Ezra continues to question and to remonstrate up through chapter 10); *2 Baruch* has more emphasis on Israel as a collective group. Even so, both texts divide up the world into the same categories of Israel and the nations; the category of Israel is further subdivided into those who keep the Law and those who do not. See for interpretation and possible relationship between the two Dereck Daschke, *City of Ruins: Mourning the Destruction of Jerusalem Through Jewish Apocalypse* (Leiden: Brill, 2010) and Lester L. Grabbe, "4 Ezra and 2 Baruch in Social and Historical Perspective," in *Fourth Ezra and Second Baruch: Reconstruction After the Fall*, eds. Matthias Henze and Gabriele Boccaccini (Leiden: Brill, 2014), 221–35.

23 The pseudo-Philo work, *Biblical Antiquities*, does not show a special interest in prophecy. It merely slightly modifies or adds to biblical stories that include prophets; but see 9.10 for Miriam's dream vision.

24 Thackeray in his 1928 Loeb translation suggests that Josephus may be referring here to *Sibylline Oracle* 4.115 which was written about 80 CE (p. 209). But the identification is not certain, and it is at least equally likely to be a passage from the Jewish Scriptures. Since making a connection to a pagan oracular figure that the Romans recognized, such as the Sibyl, would be to Josephus' advantage (his target audience being Romans), if he were indeed alluding to Sibylline oracle we might expect him to call attention to this fact; H. St. J. Thackeray, commentary to Josephus. *The Jewish War, Volume III: Books 5–7*, trans. H. St. J. Thackeray, Loeb Classical Library 210 (Cambridge, MA: Harvard University Press, 1928), 209.

25 Alexander Kulik, *3 Baruch: Greek-Slavonic Apocalypse of Baruch* (Berlin: De Gruyter, 2010), see especially 34–37.

26 Daniel C. Harlow, *The Greek Apocalypse of Baruch (3 Baruch) in Hellenistic Judaism and Early Christianity* (New York: Brill, 1996), 156–58; 206–10; Daschke, *City of Ruins,* 176–77. This text too, was redacted by Christians and preserved in Christian circles.

27 Stephen L. Cook, "Prophecy and Apocalyptic," in *The Oxford Handbook of the Prophets*, ed. Carolyn J. Sharp (Oxford: Oxford University Press, 2016), 68–69; see also by the same author, *On the Question of the "Cessation of Prophecy" in Ancient Judaism* (Tübingen: Mohr Siebeck, 2011).

28 Isaac B. Gottlieb, "Rabbinic Reception of the Prophets," in *The Oxford Handbook of the Prophets*, ed. Carolyn J. Sharp (Oxford: Oxford University Press, 2016), 403.

29 Discussed in Gottlieb, "Rabbinic Reception," 392 and 393.

30 Ibid., 403–4.

31 Jacob Neusner, "Patterns of Prophecy," in *Earliest Christianity within the Boundaries of Judaism: Essays in Honor of Bruce Chilton*, eds. Alan J. Avery-Peck, Craig A. Evans, and Jacob Neusner (Leiden: Brill, 2016), 187, 189. Illustrations of this are in 190–217 with 203–6 being good examples; 187–217; see also by the same author, *The Rabbis and the Prophets* (Lanham, MD: University Press of America, 2011).

32 Gottlieb, "Rabbinic Reception," 394–403.

33 Grabbe, "4 Ezra and 2 Baruch," 230.

34 Martin S. Jaffee, "Rabbinic Authorship as a Collective Enterprise," in *The Cambridge Companion to the Talmud and Rabbinic Literature*, eds. Charlotte Elisheva Fonrobert and Martin S. Jaffee (Cambridge: Cambridge University Press, 2007), 25. Another strain of Jewish visionary texts, the Hekhalot literature, may have been composed as early as the Late Antique period. These texts describe the ascent to heaven of early rabbinic heroes. Having passed through the seven layers of heaven, known as the hekhalot, they were granted a vision of God on his throne, and in some texts, an enhanced ability to learn and understand Torah as granted by the angel, Sar Torah, the Prince of the Torah. For a good overview of this literature, see Michael D. Swartz, "Jewish Visionary Tradition in Rabbinic Literature," in *The Cambridge Companion to the Talmud and Rabbinic Literature*,

eds. Charlotte Elisheva Fonrobert and Martin S. Jaffee (Cambridge: Cambridge University Press, 2007), 198–221.

35 Richard A. Horsley, "Popular Prophetic Movements at Time of Jesus," *Journal for the Study of the New Testament* 8.26 (1986): 3–27; see 25 n. 15.

36 Grabbe, *Judaic Religion*, 240–41.

37 Neujahr, *Predicting the Past*, 249–81; on the genre of apocalypse in general, see the many works by Collins and by Michael E. Stone.

38 Witherington, *Jesus the Seer*, 219.

Translations

Josephus. *The Jewish War, Volume II: Books 3–4*. Translated by H. St. J. Thackeray. Loeb Classical Library 487. Cambridge, MA: Harvard University Press, 1927.

Josephus. *The Jewish War, Volume III: Books 5–7*. Translated by H. St. J. Thackeray. Loeb Classical Library 210. Cambridge, MA: Harvard University Press, 1928.

Josephus. *Jewish Antiquities, Volume IX: Book 20*. Translated by Louis H. Feldman. Loeb Classical Library 456. Cambridge, MA: Harvard University Press, 1965.

New Revised Standard Version. Oxford: Oxford University Press, 2006.

Philo. *On the Confusion of Tongues. On the Migration of Abraham. Who Is the Heir of Divine Things? On Mating with the Preliminary Studies*. Translated by F. H. Colson and G. H. Whitaker. Loeb Classical Library 261. Cambridge, MA: Harvard University Press, 1932.

Philo. *On Abraham. On Joseph. On Moses*. Translated by F. H. Colson. Loeb Classical Library 289. Cambridge, MA: Harvard University Press, 1935.

Philo. *On the Decalogue: On the Special Laws, Books 1–3*. Translated by F. H. Colson. Loeb Classical Library 320. Cambridge, MA: Harvard University Press, 1937.

Priest, J. "*Testament of Moses* (First Century A.D.): A New Translation and Introduction." In *The Old Testament Pseudepigrapha*: *Volume One*: *Apocalyptic Literature and Testaments*, edited by James H. Charlesworth, 919–34. 1983. Reprint, Peabody, MA: Hendrickson, 2016.

Vermes, Geza. *The Complete Dead Sea Scrolls*. 7th ed. London: Penguin Classics, 2012.

Bibliography

Bohak, Gideon. *Ancient Jewish Magic*. Cambridge: Cambridge University Press, 2008.

Charlesworth, J. H. "*Treatise of Shem* (First Century B.C.): A New Translation and Introduction." In *The Old Testament Pseudepigrapha*: *Volume One*: *Apocalyptic Literature and Testaments*, edited by James H. Charlesworth, 473–86. 1983. Reprint, Peabody, MA: Hendrickson, 2016.

Collins, John J. *Seers, Sibyls & Sages in Hellenistic-Roman Judaism*. Leiden: E.J. Brill, 1997.

Cook, Stephen L. "Prophecy and Apocalyptic." In *The Oxford Handbook of the Prophets*, edited by Carolyn J. Sharp, 67–83. Oxford: Oxford University Press, 2016.

———. *On the Question of the "Cessation of Prophecy" in Ancient Judaism*. Tübingen: Mohr Siebeck, 2011.

Daschke, Dereck. *City of Ruins: Mourning the Destruction of Jerusalem through Jewish Apocalypse*. Leiden: Brill, 2010.

Davila, James R. "*Aramaic Levi*: A New Translation and Introduction." In *Old Testament Pseudepigrapha: More Noncanonical Scriptures: Volume One*, edited by Richard Bauckham, James R. Davila, and Alexander Panayotov, 121–42. Grand Rapids, MI: William B. Eerdmans, 2013.

———. *The Provenance of the Pseudepigrapha: Jewish, Christian, or Other?* Leiden: Brill, 2005.

Gottlieb, Isaac B. "Rabbinic Reception of the Prophets." In *The Oxford Handbook of the Prophets*, edited by Carolyn J. Sharp, 388–406. Oxford: Oxford University Press, 2016.

Grabbe, Lester L. "4 Ezra and 2 Baruch in Social and Historical Perspective." In *Fourth Ezra and Second Baruch: Reconstruction After the Fall*, edited by Matthias Henze and Gabriele Boccaccini, 221–35. Leiden: Brill, 2014.

———. *Judaic Religion in the Second Temple Period: Belief and Practice from the Exile to Yavneh*. London: Routledge, 2000.

Harlow, Daniel C. *The Greek Apocalypse of Baruch (3 Baruch) in Hellenistic Judaism and Early Christianity*. New York: Brill, 1996.

Hezser, Catherine. *Jewish Literacy in Roman Palestine*. Tübingen: Mohr Siebeck, 2001.

Horsley, Richard A. "Popular Prophetic Movements at Time of Jesus." *Journal for the Study of the New Testament* 8.26 (1986): 3–27.

Jaffee, Martin S. "Rabbinic Authorship as a Collective Enterprise." In *The Cambridge Companion to the Talmud and Rabbinic Literature*, edited by Charlotte Elisheva Fonrobert and Martin S. Jaffee, 17–37. Cambridge: Cambridge University Press, 2007.

Klijn, A.F.J. "*2 (Syriac Apocalypse of) Baruch* (Early Second Century A.D.): A New Translation and Introduction." In *The Old Testament Pseudepigrapha: Volume One: Apocalyptic Literature and Testaments*, edited by James H. Charlesworth, 615–52. 1983. Reprint, Peabody, MA: Hendrickson, 2016.

Kulik, Alexander. *3 Baruch: Greek-Slavonic Apocalypse of Baruch*. Berlin: De Gruyter, 2010.

Lightfoot, J.L. *The Sibylline Oracles: With Introduction, Translation, and Commentary on the First and Second Books*. Oxford: Oxford University Press, 2007.

Metzger, B.M. "*The Fourth Book of Ezra* (Late First Century A.D.) with the Four Additional Chapters: A New Translation and Introduction." In *The Old Testament*

Pseudepigrapha: *Volume One*: *Apocalyptic Literature and Testaments*, edited by James H. Charlesworth, 517–59. 1983. Reprint, Peabody, MA: Hendrickson, 2016.

Meyer, Elizabeth. *Legitimacy and Law in the Roman World: Tabulae in Roman Belief and Practice*. New York: Cambridge University Press, 2004.

Meyer, Marvin W. and Richard Smith, eds. *Ancient Christian Magic: Coptic Texts of Ritual Power*. Princeton, NJ: Princeton University Press, 1999.

Neujahr, Matthew. *Predicting the Past in the Ancient Near East: Mantic Historiography in Ancient Mesopotamia, Judah, and the Mediterranean World*. Providence, RI: Brown Judaic Studies, 2012.

Neusner, Jacob. "Patterns of Prophecy." In *Earliest Christianity Within the Boundaries of Judaism*: *Essays in Honor of Bruce Chilton*, edited by Alan J. Avery-Peck, Craig A. Evans, and Jacob Neusner, 187–217. Leiden: Brill, 2016.

———. *The Rabbis and the Prophets*. Lanham, MD: University Press of America, 2011.

Parke, H. W. *Sibyls and Sibylline Prophecy in Classical Antiquity*. London: Routledge, 1988.

Reed, Annette Yoshiko. *Fallen Angels and the History of Judaism and Christianity: The Reception of Enochic Literature*. Cambridge: Cambridge University Press, 2006.

Swartz, Michael D. "Jewish Visionary Tradition in Rabbinic Literature." In *The Cambridge Companion to the Talmud and Rabbinic Literature*, edited by Charlotte Elisheva Fonrobert and Martin S. Jaffee, 198–221. Cambridge: Cambridge University Press, 2007.

Thackeray, H. St. J. *Josephus. The Jewish War, Volume III: Books 5–7*. Translated by H. St. J. Thackeray, Loeb Classical Library 210. Cambridge, MA: Harvard University Press, 1928.

Vermes, Geza. *The Complete Dead Sea Scrolls*. 7th ed. London: Penguin Classics, 2012.

Witherington, Ben. *Jesus the Seer: The Progress of Prophecy*. Peabody, MA: Hendrickson, 1999.

Wright, Benjamin G. "*The Apocryphon of Ezekiel*: A New Translation and Introduction." In *Old Testament Pseudepigrapha*: *More Noncanonical Scriptures*: *Volume One*, edited by Richard Bauckham, James R. Davila, and Alexander Panayotov, 380–92. Grand Rapids, MI: William B. Eerdmans, 2013.

2 The early Christians

Prophecy, apology, and heresiology

> Now Phlegon, in the thirteenth or fourteenth book, I think, of his Chronicles, not only ascribed to Jesus a knowledge of future events . . . but also testified that the result corresponded to His predictions. So that he also, by these very admissions regarding foreknowledge, as if against his will, expressed his opinion that the doctrines taught by the fathers of our system were not devoid of divine power.
>
> (Origen, *Against Celsus* 2.14)

Phlegon of Tralles was a freedman of Emperor Hadrian who, in addition to his history, wrote books on Sicily, the topography of Rome, Roman festivals, and marvels. This passage from Phlegon (by way of Origen) indicates that some pagans among the well-connected, intellectual set understood Jesus of Nazareth to have been a prophet. Jesus' actions and message could be understood as being intentionally in line with prophets of the Jewish Scriptures or as a representative of a new type of eschatological prophet, with a focus on the in-breaking age of catastrophic (and then heavenly) change.[1] His followers saw him initially as a great prophet, and sometimes as the Messiah until they became convinced that he was in fact the Son of God. They reached this conclusion, according to early Church writings, on the basis of prophetic texts from the Jewish Scriptures. The inspired interpreter in this case was Jesus himself, more specifically, the risen Christ. The interpretation session took place on the walk to Emmaus.

> Now on that same day two of them were going to a village called Emmaus, about seven miles from Jerusalem, and talking with each other about all these things that had happened. While they were talking and discussing, Jesus himself came near and went with them, but their eyes were kept from recognizing him. And he said to them, "What are you discussing with each

> other while you walk along?" They stood still, looking sad. Then one of them, whose name was Cleopas, answered him, "Are you the only stranger in Jerusalem who does not know the things that have taken place there in these days?" He asked them, "What things?" They replied, "The things about Jesus of Nazareth, who was a prophet mighty in deed and word before God and all the people, and how our chief priests and leaders handed him over to be condemned to death and crucified him. But we had hoped that he was the one to redeem Israel" . . . Then he said to them, "Oh, how foolish you are, and how slow of heart to believe all that the prophets have declared! Was it not necessary that the Messiah should suffer these things and then enter into his glory?" Then beginning with Moses and all the prophets, he interpreted to them the things about himself in all the scriptures.
>
> (Luke 24:13–27)

Prophets, prophecy, and oracles were fundamental to Christian identity. Early Christians crafted their own identity over against that of the Jewish community by reinterpreting a shared set of prophetic texts. Like other first-century Jews, they interpreted these Scriptures as foretelling their own community and present situation and they looked to these Scriptures for information about their future. Also like them, they would appropriate pagan oracular texts, project their own history into the pagan past and use ancient Greek oracles to lend legitimacy to their new faith. Christians borrowed and adapted Jewish parabiblical writings such as we surveyed in the last chapter. They also produced their own prophetic texts: parabiblical narratives which contained visions or prophecies of Israel which pointed toward the Church and apocalypses which described a future time of crisis and then vindication, peace, and exaltation. Christians depicted themselves receiving heavenly visions. Orthodox Christians fought bitterly with other Christian groups, Valentinians, Marcionites, and Montanists over the proper interpretation of prophetic texts from the past and over the production of new prophetic writings and teachings in the present. Prophecy was used as we have seen before for appropriation and attack.

This chapter will survey the use of prophecy and oracles in Christian circles briefly from the first to the third centuries, concentrating most attention on the busy second century, a period which produced many apologies (literature of defense or attack on pagans and Jews) and heresiologies (attacks or arguments from orthodox Christians against heretics), both of which incorporated arguments about prophecy.

We will start with the many prohibitions against Christians practicing divination. In the *Didache*, an early church handbook (50–120 CE), we find a prohibition against magic, witchcraft, purifiers, astrology, and omens (*Didache* 2). In the *Ascension of Isaiah* (150–200 CE), divination is connected to other sins such as fornication (2.4). As mentioned in Chapter 1, there is late evidence (generally third century and beyond) for Christian interest in divination spells and astrology.[2]

The early church, like the Jewish community, had many prophets in the first century. Like them, prophets seem to fade out after the second century, though the numbers for the second century are fairly good as well. Both Paul in his letter to the Corinthians (1 Corinthians 12:28 and 14:1–5) and the author of the *Interpretation of Knowledge* (a text found at Nag Hammadi) refer to prophecy as a spiritual gift which is present in the community (*Interpretation of Knowledge* 15; dates to 150–200 CE). The *Didache* categorizes "prophet" among those who, like bishops and deacons, "do good service" (15). In this text, a church may or may not have a prophet (13); prophets travel and are maintained by each congregation as they pass through (13). Prophets are to be tested (false prophets preach a different doctrine and are money-hungry; their actions are not consistent with Christian teaching, 11).

Active early Christian prophets must include the apostle Paul. Although he did not call himself a prophet, he had a vision (2 Corinthians 12:1), and Eusebius, the early church historian, calls both him and Barnabas prophets (Eusebius, *Church History* 2.3.3). The apostle Philip and his daughters were prophets (Eusebius, *Church History* 3.31.5; 3.37.1). Acts mentions the prophet Agabus (Acts 11:27 and 21:10; Eusebius, *Church History* 2.3.4). Also mentioned in Acts are Simon Magus and his female follower, who the second-century heresiologists deem heretics (Acts 8:9–24). Irenaeus (*Against Heresies* 1.23.4) asserts that they use "familiars" and "dream-senders," as do the Carpocrations (1.25.3); a Nag Hammadi text (*Revelation of Peter* 74–75) accuses them of interpreting dreams falsely, and Tertullian is irate at the idea that Simon Magus and his followers claim to raise the prophets from Hades. According to Tertullian, no one can drag up the soul from there, only God! (*Treatise on the Soul* 57). Eusebius records also an early church prophet named Quadratus (see Eusebius, *Church History* 3.37.1). The New Testament book of Revelation is a visionary text. On the identity of its author, there was some debate in the early church. Dionysius, an early church father, believed that Revelation was composed by another John who was divinely inspired, not the apostle John; Justin Martyr believed it was John, the disciple of Jesus (Eusebius, *Church History* 7.25.7 and 7.25.26; 4.18.8). Aune argues that we can see evidence of active prophets in this text beyond that of the author himself.[3] Basilides, a Gnostic religious teacher in Alexandria (117 to 138 CE) had prophets attached to his movement, Barcabbas and Barcoph (Eusebius, *Church History* 4.7.7). The prophetess Philumene was attached to the Marcionites (those who rejected the God of the Jewish Scriptures and accepted a canon comprised of certain letters of Paul and parts of the Gospel of Luke; Eusebius, *Church History* 5.13.2). Tertullian accuses the Marcionites of using astrology (*Against Marcion* 1.18). The *Martyrdom of Polycarp* describes Polycarp as having been a prophetic teacher; Justin mentions that prophecy was alive in his day, as do Tertullian and Irenaeus (on Justin, see Eusebius, *Church History* 4.18.8; Tertullian: *Against Marcion* 4.22; *Treatise on the Soul* 2; Irenaeus, *Against Heresies* 2.32.4 and also 5.6.1; Eusebius, *Church History* 5.7.4, 6). The Montanists had two prophetesses, Priscilla/Prisca and Maximilla (Tertullian, *On the Resurrection of the Flesh* 11; Eusebius, *Church History* 5.14). Marcus the Valentinian and his followers, active on the Rhone, drew lots to determine who would prophesy, and were interested in numerology (Irenaeus, *Against Heresies* 1.13.3–7). And we must take up once again the evidence of Celsus, that second-century pagan author who, according to Origen, had accused the Christians of his day of a great eagerness for prophecies still coming out of the Middle East:

> But those sayings which were uttered or not uttered in Judea, after the manner of that country, as indeed they are still delivered among the people of Phoenicia and Palestine – these they look upon as marvellous sayings, and unchangeably true.
>
> (*Against Celsus* 7.3)

Laura Nasrallah, in her analysis of the divisions among second-century Christians with respect to prophecy, identifies two issues that caused disagreement. One was the method of inspiration: was prophecy ecstatic, a state in which one was utterly possessed, out of one's senses, and raving? Or was there room for the rational, controlled, part of the soul? As part of her analysis of an anonymous, second-century, anti-Montanist source (excerpted in Eusebius, *Church History* 5.16–17), Nasrallah traces the evidence for this tension across Second Temple Judaism and pagan culture, both of which groups also debated the method by which prophetic speech could take place.[4]

Another issue that active prophets raised was what Nasrallah calls the "timeline of prophecy." That is, some Christians believed that prophecy had ended with John the Baptist (see for example, Luke 16:16; *Secret Book of James* 6; *Gospel of Nicodemus*: *The Descent of Christ into Hell* 2(18)). In their view, after Christ, there was no further need for it, the full revelation of God having been fulfilled in his advent. But against this notion was the message of John and Acts, the notion of an Advocate or Paraclete that would assist the Christians in their earthly travails. Jesus had said,

> And I will ask the Father, and he will give you another Advocate, to be with you forever. This is the Spirit of truth, whom the world cannot receive, because it neither sees him nor knows him. You know him, because he abides with you, and he will be in you.
>
> (John 14:15–17)

This advocate was thought to have arrived at Pentecost when the disciples were filled with the Holy Spirit and given the ability to understand and speak in other languages (Acts 2:1–4). This event was interpreted as the fulfillment of a prophecy from the prophet Joel, from the Jewish Scriptures.

> In the last days it will be, God declares, that I will pour out my Spirit upon all flesh, and your sons and your daughters shall prophesy, and your young men shall see visions, and your old men shall dream dreams.
>
> (Acts 2:17)

The members of the Montanist group, or New Prophecy, believed that it was the present, rather than the past, that was the Golden Age of prophecy. Tertullian (who seems to identify with this group) writes that "the true system of prophecy . . . has arisen in this present age" (*Treatise on the Soul* 2; compare *On Modesty* 21).[5] In his apology directed toward pagans, Tertullian evinces a very similar attitude to that of Josephus or the Qumran community when he writes that the proof of the Scriptures is to be found in the fulfillment of them which is taking place then and there, before their very eyes:

> If you doubt that they are as ancient as we say, we offer proof that they are divine. And you may convince yourselves of this at once, and without going very far. Your instructors, the world, and the age, and the event, are all before you. All that is taking place around you was fore-announced; all that you now see with your eye was previously heard by the ear. The swallowing up of cities by the earth; . . . the collision of kingdoms with kingdoms . . . the exaltation of the lowly, and the humbling of the proud; . . . it was all foreseen and predicted before it came to pass. While we suffer the calamities, we read of them in the Scriptures; as we examine, they are proved. Well, the truth of a prophecy, I think, is the demonstration of its being from above. Hence there is among us an assured faith in regard to coming events as things already

> proved to us, for they were predicted along with what we have day by day fulfilled. They are uttered by the same voices, they are written in the same books – the same Spirit inspires them. All time is one to prophecy foretelling the future. Among men, it may be, a distinction of times is made while the fulfilment is going on: from being future we think of it as present, and then from being present we count it as belonging to the past. How are we to blame, I pray you, that we believe in things to come as though they already were, with the grounds we have for our faith in these two steps?
>
> (*Apology* 20)

In this statement by Tertullian, he expresses a sentiment that we see again and again in second-century Christian authors: the fulfillment of prophecies is sure proof. Justin Martyr, in his *First Apology* 30 (written approximately 150 CE), writes:

> But lest any one should meet us with the question, What should prevent that He whom we call Christ, being a man born of men, performed what we call His mighty works by magical art, and by this appeared to be the Son of God? We will now offer proof, not trusting mere assertions, but being of necessity persuaded by those who prophesied [of Him] before these things came to pass, for with our own eyes we behold things that have happened and are happening just as they were predicted.

Here he, like Tertullian, points to the present age, the events of his own day, as evidence of the fulfillment of these ancient Jewish prophecies. Tatian (160–170 CE), in his *Address to the Greeks* 29, asserts that he was converted by reading the simple, prophetic writings of the Christians; we see a similar sentiment in Theophilus of Antioch:

> Therefore, do not be sceptical, but believe; for I myself also used to disbelieve that this would take place, but now, having taken these things into consideration, I believe. At the same time, I met with the sacred Scriptures of the holy prophets, who also by the Spirit of God foretold the things that have already happened, just as they came to pass, and the things now occurring as they are now happening, and things future in the order in which they shall be accomplished. Admitting, therefore, the proof which events happening as predicted afford, I do not disbelieve, but I believe.
>
> (*To Autolycus* 1.14; compare Luke 24:13–27 and the *Preaching of Peter* 6.15; 100–150 CE)

The prophecies which have been fulfilled in these cases are the Jewish Scriptures, but some Christians argued that their present time, and the Christian Church, were the fulfillment of pagan prophecies as well (specifically oracles of the Sibyl, as in the writings of Theophilus of Antioch and Clement of Alexandria, discussed below; other pagan oracular figures would be appropriated as well; see Chapter 3 for the continuance of this practice among third-century Christians).

Christians understood the Jewish Scriptures to contain prophecies and hints, types and allegories, that were intended to foretell a Messiah, Jesus of Nazareth, a Suffering Servant, who through his suffering would redeem humankind.[6] There were two advents of Christ. The first had already happened, resulting in the crucifixion, resurrection, and inauguration of the Church. The second was to come in the future. This was foretold also in the Jewish Scriptures as well as in the New Testament text, Revelation, which depicted the course of events in the last days. Parabiblical texts, some of them taken over from the Jewish population such as were discussed in Chapter 1 (for example, *Enoch* or the *Testaments of the Twelve Patriarchs*), featured individuals from the Jewish Scriptures who predicted a future vindication of the righteous and punishment of the wicked, much as we saw in Second Temple Judaism. (An example of this would be the *Apocalypse of Abraham*, which dates to the first or second century CE. In this text, Abraham is taken on a tour and he sees the past and future of Israel; God gives him a description of the end times.) Other writings of this type featured individuals from the New Testament such as the second-century text, the *Gospel of Mary*, in which text Mary appears to describe a vision of the soul that she received from the Lord.[7]

In what follows we will examine the role that prophecy played for orthodox Christians in the second century, in establishing their relationship with three groups: Jews, Gnostic Christians (touched on earlier), and pagans.

In the *Gospel of Thomas*, the disciples say to Christ, "Twenty-four prophets have spoken in Israel, and they all spoke of you" (52; dates to 50–140 or at least to before 200 CE).[8] Several of the early church fathers discuss methods of scriptural interpretation, and the *Gospel of Peter* provides a good example of how this worked: "And they crucified him; and parted his garments, casting lots: that it might be fulfilled which was spoken by the prophet, 'They parted my garments among them, and upon my vesture did they cast lots'" (35; 70–160 CE). In this example, Psalms 22:18 is quoted, and it is explained that these events happened in the life of Christ. Some Christians believed that not all prophetical texts could bear this type of literal reading. Tertullian in *Against Marcion* addresses this issue explaining how prophecies may be written in a variety of ways, and the reader must not be thrown by this (3.5, 13, 18).

Many early Christian writers wrote defensively, sometimes aggressively so, of their interpretation of Jewish Scriptures, taking great pains to explain how each point of the Christian creed could be detected in them. The life and nature of Christ and his two advents were not the only topics, however. The end of the Mosaic Law, the triumph of the Church over Judaism, and the nature of the future Jerusalem after the end-time events, these were regular subjects of discussion and exegesis.

For Justin Martyr, who will serve as an illustrating example, prophets are the only sure way to the truth (*Dialogue with Trypho* 8). In the present time of the Church, the gift of prophecy has passed from Jews to Christians (*Dialogue with Trypho* 51, 82, 87). And the Christians are the superior interpreters of prophecies from the Jewish Scriptures. Justin works to demonstrate this particularly in *1 Apology* and *Dialogue with Trypho*. In *1 Apology* 32, Justin demonstrates that Moses predicted Christ. In 33–35 he points to passages in Isaiah, Zechariah, and Micah, to prove that specific details of Christ's life were foretold, including the place of his birth. According to Justin, both Jews and Christians believe that the prophets expressed themselves in "parables and types" (*Dialogue with Trypho* 90). But the Jews, according to Justin, do not apply these methods correctly: they read the text literally when they should interpret non-literally (*Dialogue with Trypho* 14, 42, 94, 112; *1 Apology* 36). The interpretation of the serpent of bronze, raised up by Moses in the wilderness (Numbers 21:9; 1 Kings 18:4) is taken up by Justin in *Dialogue* 94–109 (see also John 3:14; *Epistle of Barnabas* 12.5–7; Tertullian, *Against the Jews* 10.10). This passage is given such priority because, Justin says, it is a text that both Jews and Christians believed referred to the Messiah (*Dialogue with Trypho* 110). Justin derides the "foolish" interpretation which the Jewish teachers apply to this Scripture and seeks to demonstrate that only a symbolic interpretation makes sense (*Dialogue with Trypho* 112; compare 65, in which Justin corrects the interpretation of Isaiah 42:8, which he says the Jews read without due reference to the context; compare Plutarch, *How to Read Poetry*; Tertullian, *Against the Jews* 9.2).

One common argument found in the writings of Justin Martyr is that the Scriptures refer to two different advents of the Messiah (or Christ). In the first advent the Messiah will appear as a Suffering Servant; at the end of time he will return to the earth in glory (Justin Martyr, *Dialogue with Trypho* 40, 49, 52, 110, 111; a similar "two advents" appears in interpretation in Tertullian, *Against the Jews* 14.1–11).

The abrogation of Mosaic Law is another theme. In *Dialogue with Trypho* 13–23, Justin takes up in succession the regulations of Mosaic Law and shows via Scripture why it is no longer necessary to observe these (sacrifice (13); unleavened bread (14); circumcision (16)). Justin provides different reasons for the redundancy of Mosaic Law. The Law was given because the people were sinful (*Dialogue with Trypho* 21–23) or in the case of circumcision, it was given to the Hebrews to mark them out for future punishment (*Dialogue with Trypho* 16, 19; 44; the idea is reflected in Tertullian, *Against the Jews* 3). Elsewhere the Mosaic Law was but a type or symbol of the true wishes of God (42; compare 14). The *Epistle of Barnabas* also relies on Scripture to establish the end of Mosaic Law (2.4–10; 3.1–6; 9.1–10.12; 15.2–9) and supersessionism is evident throughout this work (but see especially 4.6–14; 13.1–14.9). To this we can compare Tertullian, *Against the Jews*, which has a similar concern to establish the redundancy of Mosaic Law (2–6) and a strong supersessionist message (1, 3, 6, 11–14). In Justin's view, the majority of Jews are going to reject Christ as was foretold in Scriptures (*Dialogue with Trypho* 120; *1 Apology* 49; compare Tertullian, *Against the Jews* 11.11 and 13.28; *Apology* 21; *Against Marcion*, Book 3).

Many apocalypses and other writings which contained visions were found in a collection of thirteen codices at Nag Hammadi, a town in upper Egypt. It is not quite clear who was reading and composing these texts. There is some evidence to suggest that not every individual or group who read these texts were separatists; some readers may have belonged to an orthodox congregation that did not include these writings among its most sacred texts or for whom these texts played but a minor, supplementary, role to that of the emerging canon. Their find-spot, near the site of a Pachomian monastery, may indicate that they once belonged to the monks themselves. As we will see, some orthodox Christians did object strenuously to the theology reflected in some of the writings found at Nag Hammadi.

In Irenaeus' *Against Heresies*, Irenaeus constructs a genealogical relationship between non-orthodox Christians, or heretics, as he calls them. Irenaeus begins his heresiology by taking up the Valentinians, with their founder Valentinus and his successor, Ptolemy, but he later asserts that all heretics were connected in some way to Simon Magus, the magician mentioned in Acts. In his preface Irenaeus claims that he spoke with followers of Valentinians and that he had read Valentinian writings; he relates also that Marcus was operating near him on the Rhone (1.13.7); and yet his descriptions of Gnostic teachings do not match up precisely with what we find at Nag Hammadi. There is a great variety in these texts, even in groups that we can more or less comfortably identify as belonging to a specific type of Gnostic Christianity, such as

Valentinian. This raises questions about the depth of Irenaeus' knowledge of Gnostics as well as the umbrella terms that he applies to them (Valentinians, Ophites, Sethians) and other orthodox Christians who adopt his terms. Here we propose only to outline in broad terms what he saw as the abuse of prophecy and the prophetic writings.

Some heretics, such as Marcion, Irenaeus describes as denigrating the God of the Jewish Scriptures altogether and crafting a new set of Scriptures.

> Marcion of Pontus succeeded him, and developed his doctrine. In so doing, he advanced the most daring blasphemy against Him who is proclaimed as God by the law and the prophets, declaring Him to be the author of evils, to take delight in war, to be infirm of purpose, and even to be contrary to Himself. But Jesus being derived from that father who is above the God that made the world, and coming into Judaea in the times of Pontius Pilate the governor, who was the procurator of Tiberius Caesar, was manifested in the form of a man to those who were in Judaea, abolishing the prophets and the law, and all the works of that God who made the world, whom also he calls Cosmocrator. Besides this, he mutilates the Gospel which is according to Luke, removing all that is written respecting the generation of the Lord, and setting aside a great deal of the teaching of the Lord, in which the Lord is recorded as most clearly confessing that the Maker of this universe is His Father. He likewise persuaded his disciples that he himself was more worthy of credit than are those apostles who have handed down the Gospel to us, furnishing them not with the Gospel, but merely a fragment of it. In like manner, too, he dismembered the Epistles of Paul, removing all that is said by the apostle respecting that God who made the world, to the effect that He is the Father of our Lord Jesus Christ, and also those passages from the prophetical writings which the apostle quotes, in order to teach us that they announced beforehand the coming of the Lord.
>
> (*Against Heresies* 1.27.2)

The Christian author Rhodon, who died about 180 CE, is described in Eusebius, *Church History* 5.13.6 as an opponent of a Marcionite teacher, one Apelles, who taught that the prophecies (and here he is referring to the Jewish Scriptures) were wrong and self-contradictory. For Apelles, prophecy was in the present, in human form, in the person of the Marcionite prophet Philumene. For such groups (see also Simon Magus' followers, Saturninus from Antioch, Basilides from Alexandria, and Carpocrates, 1.23.3; 1.24.2 and 5; 1.25.3), the prophetic texts that orthodox Christianity relies upon were simply rejected. For those that did accept the Jewish Scriptures, Irenaeus complains that they interpret the words of the evangelists, apostles, Law and the Prophets so as to support their own ideas (1.3.6). A good example of how this works is found at *Against Heresies* 2.22.1–2 and following: according to Irenaeus, these heretics misunderstand Isaiah 61:2. They interpret this text in such a way as to help them calculate that Christ was thirty when he was baptized. Thus, they see thirty as a symbolic number, the number of Aeons or cosmic realms in their (non-orthodox) conception of the universe. Heretics, Irenaeus asserts, think that the Scriptures are ambiguous and that one needs to use outside information to make sense of them (3.2.1). To Irenaeus, the real meaning of Scripture is clear to all and not ambiguous (2.271–73). The way to interpret them properly has been made clear through the tradition which has been received through the apostolic succession (3.2.2; 3.4.2; 4.33; compare Tertullian, *Prescription against Heretics* 20–21; 28). Irenaeus also repeatedly makes the claim that some Gnostic groups attributed the Jewish prophetical writings to different types of cosmic beings (1.7.3; 1.30.10–11; 4.35). There is a three-part division of Scripture in the Valentinian text, Ptolemy's *Letter to Flora*, though it does not align precisely with Irenaeus' generalizing statements.

Excerpts from Theodotus 24 asserts that the Valentinians believed that the prophetic spirit had been poured out onto the Church. Epiphanius, *Panarion* 39.5.1 (lived approximately 310–320 to 403 CE) writes that the Gnostic "Sethians" had produced many pseudepigraphical writings in the names of Old Testament figures (compare 26.8). In the *Apocalypse* or *Revelation of Adam*, for example, which dates to end of the first or beginning of the second century CE, Adam recounts a dream vision to his son, Seth. Seth is a special child, the only one of Adam's offspring to have within him the divine spark. It is his descendants, "the holy seed," who have the capability of connecting with the divine. The vision provides Seth with the true knowledge of who he is and how the universe works: throughout time there has been a persistent struggle between the genuine divine forces and the creator god; in the future, a heavenly illuminator of knowledge will come (this is the Christ figure) who will redeem the souls of the elect. But we also see among the Gnostic collection at Nag Hammadi pseudepigraphical writings in the names of New Testament figures that reference visions received or that describe the contents of such visions. The *Revelation of Paul* provides a description of Paul's vision and ascent to the tenth heaven, which he had mentioned in 2 Corinthians. This type of additional, secret revelation that went beyond what was disclosed in the New Testament was abhorrent to the orthodox. Tertullian in the *Prescription against Heretics* objects that Paul himself indicates that he was not allowed to give the details of his vision and if he could not, then how should anyone else? (24).

Irenaeus in *Against Heresies* notes that it is harder to convert the Gentiles because they did not accept the Jewish Scriptures, which Christians could show had been fulfilled (4.24.2). In the second-century writings which deal with pagan oracles, there are two main approaches exhibited. The first is negative: oracles came from daemons (Athenagoras 27; Tertullian, *Apology* 22; *Treatise on the Soul* 1; 46; Tatian's *Address to the Greeks* 12; compare Tertullian, *Treatise on the Soul* 47 and Origen, *Against Celsus* 4.92). The *Octavius* of Minucius Felix (160–250 CE) is a dialogue, and it gives us the perspective of a pagan and arguments in support of pagan prophecy, as well as the Christian answer to these arguments. The pagan point of view is this: when in the past pagan prophecies were scoffed at or ignored, it always led to disaster (7). In this dialogue, however, this argument is brushed aside, and the Christian viewpoint at the end of the day is triumphant. The Christian speaker explains how daemons operate pagan oracles:

> These impure spirits, therefore – the demons – as is shown by the Magi, by the philosophers, and by Plato, consecrated under statues and images, lurk there, and by their afflatus attain the authority as of a present deity; while in the meantime they are breathed into the prophets, while they dwell in the shrines, while sometimes they animate the fibres of the entrails, control the flights of birds, direct the lots, are the cause of oracles involved in many falsehoods. For they are both deceived, and they deceive; inasmuch as they are both ignorant of the simple truth, and for their own ruin they confess not that which they know. Thus they weigh men downwards from heaven, and call them away from the true God to material things.
>
> (Minucius Felix, *Octavius* 27)

Christian authors will also on occasion try to make the argument from antiquity; that is, they will argue that ancient Jewish prophets (who, in their view, belonged properly to the Christian Church) had preceded pagan ones, making Christian prophecy older and therefore better (see for example, Origen, *Against Celsus* 7.4). Christian authors also occasionally argue that pagan oracles are faked (Hippolytus, *Refutation of All Heresies* Book 4) or defunct (Clement of Alexandria, *Exhortation to the Heathen* 2). These last two were both weak arguments, as the pagans did have quite old oracles which the

Christians wished to employ to legitimize the existence of their own community. Furthermore, as will be discussed in Chapter 3, though some oracles seem to have declined, overall, across the Empire, pagans did have a vibrant oracular tradition through the third century. Perhaps for this reason the second common trend that we see among second-century Christians who are writing about pagan oracles, is to appeal to the evidence of the pagan Sibyl to support the Christian faith. The Sibylline oracles that the Christians quoted were not in actuality pagan prophecies at all – they were instead the Jewish *Sibylline Oracles*, now with added, Christian, interpolations (though this was not admitted, or perhaps not even recognized, at the time). For these Christian authors, a quote from "the Sibyl" served as the clincher:

> For they predicted also pestilences, and famines, and wars. And there was not one or two, but many, at various times and seasons among the Hebrews; and also among the Greeks there was the Sibyl; and they all have spoken things consistent and harmonious with each other, both what happened before them and what happened in their own time, and what things are now being fulfilled in our own day: wherefore we are persuaded also concerning the future things that they will fall out, as also the first have been accomplished.
>
> (Theophilus of Antioch, *To Autolycus* 2.9; see also 2.31)

Clement of Alexandria (182–202 CE) goes even further than this when he equates the truth to be found in the Sibyl with that found in the Jewish Scriptures, and categorizes both of these "oracles" as the path to salvation:

> It is now time, as we have dispatched in order the other points, to go to the prophetic Scriptures; for the oracles present us with the appliances necessary for the attainment of piety, and so establish the truth. The divine Scriptures and institutions of wisdom form the short road to salvation. Devoid of embellishment, of outward beauty of diction, of wordiness and seductiveness, they raise up humanity strangled by wickedness, teaching men to despise the casualties of life; and with one and the same voice remedying many evils, they at once dissuade us from pernicious deceit, and clearly exhort us to the attainment of the salvation set before us. Let the Sibyl prophetess, then, be the first to sing to us the song of salvation: –
>
> So He is all sure and unerring:
> Come, follow no longer darkness and gloom;

> See, the sun's sweet-glancing light shines gloriously.
> Know, and lay up wisdom in your hearts:
> There is one God, who sends rains, and winds, and earthquakes,
> Thunderbolts, famines, plagues, and dismal sorrows,
> And snows and ice. But why detail particulars?
> He reigns over heaven, He rules earth,
> He truly is; –
> (Clement of Alexandria, *Exhortation to the Heathen* 8)

This identification of oracular texts as a means of salvation we will see again in the pagan authors of the third century; Josephus, too, had expressed a similar idea (*Jewish Wars* 6.310–15).

By the second century, Christianity, a religion that had its origins in new interpretations of prophetic writings, was conflicted over the proper role of prophecy and prophets. New subdivisions of the faith had arisen whose prophets claimed to receive revelations that did not always match those of the emerging orthodox canon. Visionary literature continued to be produced, and many new pseudepigraphic works claimed the authority of figures from the history of Israel and from the apostolic age of the Church. Orthodox Christians began to take a keen interest in defining and defending their identity over against Jews, pagans, and non-orthodox Christians. They attacked Jews for being poor interpreters of prophetic texts, and pagans for having daemon-led oracles, and they appropriated the oracles of both groups, adapting them to create a new body of prophetic texts that pointed to their own community and promised them a blessed future.

Notes

1 R. David Kaylor, *Jesus the Prophet: His Vision of the Kingdom on Earth* (Louisville, KY: Westminster John Knox Press, 1994); Dale B. Martin, "Jesus in Jerusalem: Armed and Not Dangerous," *Journal for the Study of the New Testament* 27.1 (2014): 3–24; Ben Witherington, *Jesus the Seer: The Progress of Prophecy* (Peabody, MA: Hendrickson, 1999), 246–92.

2 See Marvin W. Meyer and Richard Smith, eds., *Ancient Christian Magic: Coptic Texts of Ritual Power* (Princeton, NJ: Princeton University Press, 1999); Anne-Marie Luijendijk, *Forbidden Oracles? The Gospel of the Lots of Mary* (Tübingen: Mohr Siebeck, 2014).

3 David E. Aune, in his collected essays, "The Prophetic Circle of John of Patmos and the Exegesis of Revelation 22:16," 250–60 argues that Revelation 22:9 and 22:16 point to a circle of prophets and that the Jezebel figure also refers to a prophet active in that time.

4 Laura Nasrallah, *An Ecstasy of Folly: Prophecy and Authority in Early Christianity* (Cambridge, MA: Harvard University Press, 2004).
5 Paul believes that only in the future will there be full knowledge; Epiphanius' earlier anti-New Prophecy source thinks that the highpoint of prophecy was in the past; Tertullian and the adherents of the New Prophecy believe that the highpoint is now; see discussion in Nasrallah, *Ecstasy of Folly*, 93–94; on the New Prophecy and the Montanists, see also C. Trevett, *Montanism: Gender, Authority and New Prophecy* (Cambridge: Cambridge University Press, 1996), sources: 3–5; terminology: 2; geographical spread: 46–76; teachings of: 141–50.
6 See for example, Tertullian, *Against Marcion* 3.5, 13, 18.
7 For introduction, translation, and commentary, see Karen L. King in *The Nag Hammadi Scriptures: The Revised and Updated Translation of Sacred Gnostic Texts Complete in One Volume*, eds. Marvin W. Meyer and James M. Robinson (New York: HarperCollins, 2009), 737–48.
8 Translation taken from Karen L. King, "*The Gospel of Thomas* with the *Greek Gospel of Thomas*," in *The Nag Hammadi Scriptures: The Revised and Updated Translation of Sacred Gnostic Texts Complete in One Volume*, trans. Marvin W. Meyer; eds. Marvin W. Meyer and James M. Robinson (New York: HarperCollins, 2009).

Translations

The Apostolic Fathers – Justin Martyr – Irenaeus. Translated by Alexander Roberts. Edited by Alexander Roberts and James Donaldson. Revised and chronologically arranged with brief prefaces and occasional notes by A. Cleveland Coxe. Ante-Nicene Fathers 1. New York: Christian Literature, 1885.

Fathers of the Second Century: Hermas, Tatian, Athenagoras, Theophilus, and Clement of Alexandria (Entire). Translated by Marcus Dods. Edited by Alexander Roberts and James Donaldson. Revised and chronologically arranged with brief prefaces and occasional notes by A. Cleveland Coxe. Ante-Nicene Fathers 2. New York: Christian Literature, 1885.

Fathers of the Third Century: Tertullian, Part Fourth; Minucius Felix; Commodian; Origen, Part First and Second. Translated by Frederick Crombie. Edited by Alexander Roberts and James Donaldson. Revised and chronologically arranged with brief prefaces and occasional notes by A. Cleveland Coxe. Ante-Nicene Fathers 4. New York: Christian Literature, 1885.

The Gospel of Peter, the Diatessaron of Tatian, the Apocalypse of Peter, the Vision of Paul, the Apocalypse of the Virgin and Sedrach, the Testament of Abraham, the Acts of Xanthippe and Polyxena, the Narrative of Zosimus, the Apology of Aristides, the Epistles of Clement (Complete Text), Origen's Commentary of John, Books 1–10, and Commentary on Matthew, Books 1, 2, and 10–14. Translated by J. Armitage Robinson. Edited by Alexander Roberts and James Donaldson. Revised and Chronologically arranged with brief prefaces and occasional notes by A. Cleveland Coxe. Ante-Nicene Fathers 9. New York: Christian Literature, 1896–97.

King, Karen L. "*The Gospel of Thomas* with the *Greek Gospel of Thomas*." In *The Nag Hammadi Scriptures: The Revised and Updated Translation of Sacred Gnostic Texts Complete in One Volume*. Translated by Marvin W. Meyer. Edited by Marvin W. Meyer and James M. Robinson. New York: HarperCollins, 2009.

Latin Christianity: Its Founder, Tertullian. Translated by S. Thelwall. Edited by Alexander Roberts and James Donaldson. Revised and chronologically arranged with brief prefaces and occasional notes by A. Cleveland Coxe. Ante-Nicene Fathers 3. New York: Christian Literature, 1885.

New Revised Standard Version. Oxford: Oxford University Press, 2006.

Bibliography

Aune, David E. *Apocalypticism, Prophecy, and Magic in Early Christianity*. Grand Rapids, MI: Baker Academic, 2006.

Kaylor, R. David. *Jesus the Prophet: His Vision of the Kingdom on Earth*. Louisville, KY: Westminster John Knox Press, 1994.

King, Karen L. "The *Gospel of Mary* with the Greek *Gospel of Mary*." In *The Nag Hammadi Scriptures: The Revised and Updated Translation of Sacred Gnostic Texts Complete in One Volume*, edited by Marvin W. Meyer and James M. Robinson, 737–48. New York: HarperCollins, 2009.

Luijendijk, AnneMarie. *Forbidden Oracles? The Gospel of the Lots of Mary*. Tübingen: Mohr Siebeck, 2014.

Meyer, Marvin W. and Richard Smith, eds. *Ancient Christian Magic: Coptic Texts of Ritual Power*. Princeton, NJ: Princeton University Press, 1999.

Nasrallah, Laura. *An Ecstasy of Folly: Prophecy and Authority in Early Christianity*. Cambridge, MA: Harvard University Press, 2004.

Trevett, C. *Montanism: Gender, Authority and New Prophecy*. Cambridge: Cambridge University Press, 1996.

Witherington, Ben. *Jesus the Seer: The Progress of Prophecy*. Peabody, MA: Hendrickson, 1999.

3 The Greco-Romans

Pagan oracles and Christian persecution

> Nor is it only one single mode of divination that has been employed in public and in private. For, to say nothing of other nations, how many our own people have embraced!
>
> (Cicero, *On Divination* 1.2)

In a second-century dialogue composed by the Christian author, Minucius Felix (discussed in Chapter 2), the Roman perspective is set out.

> Nor yet by chance (for I would venture in the meantime even to take for granted the point in debate, and so to err on the safe side) have our ancestors succeeded in their undertakings either by the observance of auguries, or by consulting the entrails, or by the institution of sacred rites, or by the dedication of temples. Consider what is the record of books. You will at once discover that they have inaugurated the rites of all kinds of religions, either that the divine indulgence might be rewarded, or that the threatening anger might be averted, or that the wrath already swelling and raging might be appeased. . . . Thence therefore the prophets, filled with the god, and mingled with him, collect futurity beforehand, give caution for dangers, medicine for diseases, hope for the afflicted, help to the wretched, solace to calamities, alleviation to labours.
>
> (Minucius Felix, *Octavius* 7)

In the Roman Empire, for the Romans and for the cultures with which they came into contact, there were a variety of types of divination and a variety of terms by which to designate operators or practitioners. The following brief overview is not exhaustive but will provide an idea of the types of divination that were available throughout the Empire. Its purpose is to demonstrate the ubiquity of divination in pagan imperial culture so as to set pagan uses of, attitudes toward, and discourse about prophets, prophecy, and oracles in its larger context. The overview concentrates on the evidence for Greco-Roman divination.

We will start with the oracles. There were oracular centers for healing as well as for questions. Inquiries were submitted on behalf of states and on behalf of individuals. Oracular centers provided answers through several means including the spoken word (in which a prophet or prophetess spoke for the god), incubation (in which the god communicated to the inquirer via dreams), lot, dice, and mirrors.

Cicero describes lot oracles and also a division between types of divination, those that are the product of learned skill and those that are the product of divine inspiration:

> I agree, therefore, with those who have said that there are two kinds of divination: one, which is allied with art; the other, which is devoid of art. Those diviners employ art, who, having learned the known by observation, seek the unknown by deduction. On the other hand those do without art who, unaided by reason or deduction or by signs which have been observed and recorded, forecast the future while under the influence of mental excitement, or of some free and unrestrained emotion. This condition often occurs to men while dreaming and sometimes to persons who prophesy while in a frenzy – like Bacis of Boeotia, Epimenides of Crete and the Sibyl of Erythraea. In this latter class must be placed oracles – not oracles given by means of "equalized lots" – but those uttered under the impulse of divine inspiration; although divination by lot is not in itself to be despised, if it has the sanction of antiquity.
>
> (Cicero, *On Divination* 1.18)

Pausanias describes the dice oracles of Heracles in Achaea, wherein a statue is inscribed with oracles.

> On descending from Bura towards the sea you come to a river called Buraicus, and to a small Heracles in a cave. He too is surnamed Buraicus, and here one can divine by means of a tablet and dice. He who inquires of the god offers up a prayer in front of the image, and after the prayer he takes four dice, a plentiful supply of which are placed by Heracles, and

> throws them upon the table. For every figure made by the dice there is an explanation expressly written on the tablet.
>
> (Pausanias 7.25.10)

Pausanias, again, describes also the use of a mirror in the oracle at Patrae at the sanctuary of Demeter.

> Here there is an infallible oracle, not indeed for everything, but only in the case of sick folk. They tie a mirror to a fine cord and let it down, judging the distance so that it does not sink deep into the spring, but just far enough to touch the water with its rim. Then they pray to the goddess and burn incense, after which they look into the mirror, which shows them the patient either alive or dead.
>
> (Pausanias 7.21.12)

Incubation oracles were oracular centers in which the inquirer slept overnight and the god brought an answer to the inquiry in a dream (at Anariace, see Strabo 11.7.1; oracle of Ino-Pasiphaë at Thalamae, Pausanias 3.26.1).[1] There were incubation oracles associated with healing at Amphiarus (Pausanius 1.34.5), and Daunia (Strabo 6.3.9), and Epidaurus.

> In Daunia, on a hill by the name of Drium, are to be seen two hero-temples: one, to Calchas, on the very summit, where those who consult the oracle sacrifice to his shade a black ram and sleep in the hide, and the other, to Podaleirius, down near the base of the hill, this temple being about one hundred stadia distant from the sea; and from it flows a stream which is a cure-all for diseases of animals.
>
> (Strabo 6.3.9)

Aristides, a second-century philosopher and orator, records his consultations of the incubation oracle of Aesclepius at Epidaurus in a five-volume work, *Sacred Tales*, which is full of dreams, and of enthusiasm for the god, who commanded him to write down his dreams (2.2).

The famous oracles of Apollo from the archaic and classical age at Didyma and Claros were still going strong in the Roman imperial period, despite occasional statements to the contrary. Evidence of Roman imperial use and popularity for these sites has been established through the archaeological and epigraphic record, discussed at length by Parke, *Oracles of Apollo in Asia*

Minor, Strabo describes the Didyma oracular site as still enjoying a vibrant income:

> Next after the Poseidium of the Milesians, eighteen stadia inland, is the oracle of Apollo Didymeus among the Branchidae. It was set on fire by Xerxes, as were also the other temples, except that at Ephesus. The Branchidae gave over the treasures of the god to the Persian king, and accompanied him in his flight in order to escape punishment for the robbing and the betrayal of the temple. But later the Milesians erected the largest temple in the world, though on account of its size it remained without a roof. At any rate, the circuit of the sacred enclosure holds a village settlement; and there is a magnificent sacred grove both inside and outside the enclosure; and other sacred enclosures contain the oracle and the shrines. Here is laid the scene of the myth of Branchus and the love of Apollo. The temple is adorned with costliest offerings consisting of early works of art.
>
> (Strabo 14.1.5)

Imperial visits and benefactions were made at Didyma. Inscriptions dating from the second and third centuries indicate consultations by both cities and individuals about careers, contracts, oaths, cult (the proper way to worship, cult officials, the proper placement of altars), unexplained disasters, a miraculous act by the God on behalf of the local inhabitants during a Gothic attack, and philosophical discussions about the soul.[2] Claros' oracle was visited by numerous embassies from Greek cities in the second and third centuries as well as by individuals and was consulted even by Caracalla (on which see Cassius Dio 77.15.5; 16.8).[3] Recorded oracular responses indicate that inquiries were broadly similar to those at Didyma and included questions about crops, health, natural disasters, and the nature of the god.[4]

The oracle at Olympia was likely defunct by the Roman imperial period.[5] The oracle at Dodona, which was operated through several mediums (including that of a talking oak tree, talking birds, lots, a prophetess, a sacred fountain, and the ringing tones of a cauldron), Strabo describes as being "virtually extinct" (Strabo 7.7.9; compare Clement of Alexandria, *Exhortation to the Greeks* 2), though a reference in Lucan's *Pharsalia* indicates that it was perhaps still operating (Lucan 6.425).[6] Similarly, Plutarch, a priest at Delphi, wrote a work in which the participants discuss the decline of oracles in general and at Delphi (*On the Obsolescence of Oracles* 411e–f/5). But though this site was not as popular as it had been, it, too, was not totally defunct, as we can see in the following passage which mentions that there are yet some oracles being produced.

> For my part, I will never give up the survival of the soul until some second Heracles makes off with the tripod of the Pythia and abolishes and destroys the oracle; but so long as many responses are delivered even in our day of the kind that the Naxian Coraxa is said to have received, it would be impious to pass sentence of death upon the soul.
>
> (*On the Delays of Divine Vengeance* 560D)

Iamblichus' third-century text, *On the Mysteries*, also refers to the Pythian oracle at Delphi as if it were still operational. Compare Strabo on the oracle of Ammon in Libya:

> Now that I have already said much about Ammon, I wish to add only this: Among the ancients both divination in general and oracles were held in greater honour, but now great neglect of them prevails, since the Romans are satisfied with the oracles of Sibylla, and with Tyrrhenian prophecies obtained by means of the entrails of animals, flight of birds, and omens from the sky.
>
> (17.1.43)

But Diodorus Siculus writing about the same time describes an oracle that is still operative. At the oracle of Ammon in Egypt the cult statue was used as a medium of divination (Diodorus Siculus 17.50.6).[7] At Heliopolis, a major cult center in northern Syria, Lucian describes how the cult statue of Apollo there was an instrument of divination. Shaking and sweating, the statue was borne by his priests, whose movements were directed by it and interpreted by them. The movement of the statue was understood as the oracular response given to the query put by the high priest (*On the Syrian Goddess* 36).[8]

Pausanias in his *Description of Greece* mentions several other oracles that were still operational. In Book One, describing the land of "Oropus, between Attica and the land of Tanagra," he describes the oracle of Amphilochus at Mallus in Cilicia "which is the most trustworthy of my day" (1.34.3). He describes the dream oracle at Amphiaraus (1.34.5); an oracle of Night at Megaris (1.40.6); and an oracle in Argos, the citadel of Laris:

> Oracular responses are still given here, and the oracle acts in the following way. There is a woman who prophesies, being debarred from intercourse

> with a man. Every month a lamb is sacrificed at night, and the woman, after tasting the blood, becomes inspired by the god.
>
> (2.24.1)

Close to Cyaneae by Lycia, there was an oracle of Apollo Thyrxeus (7.21.13); and there was an oracle of Trophonius at Lebadeia which he describes in great detail (9.39.4–14).

Other scattered literary references allow us to add to this list. Tacitus describes Titus' visit to an oracle of Aphrodite at Paphos (Tacitus, *Histories* 2.3–4); Suetonius describes a lot oracle with dice at Geryon at Patavium (Suetonius, *Life of Tiberius* 14.3) and Vespasian's visit to an oracle at Carmel in Judea (*Life of Vespasian* 5.6). In Dio Chrysostom's hometown of Prusa, the god had foretold the ascension of Trajan (*Oration* 45.4). Pliny the Younger visited an oracle of a river god, Clitumnus, in Umbria (*Letters* 8.8.5–7). Livy mentions an oracle of Apollo which the Roman troops passed by at Hiera Comê in the second century BCE, and the wording implies that it was still active in his day (Livy 38.13.1). Parke (*Oracles of Apollo in Asia Minor*) discusses the evidence for an oracle of Apollo at Chalcedon;[9] for an oracle of Apollo Smintheus at Chryse;[10] for an oracle of Apollo at Hierapolis in Phrygia;[11] and for an oracle of Apollo at Patara in Lycia.[12] New oracles could be set up by individuals, including emperors. According to Eusebius (*Church History* 4.8.2), Hegesippus recorded that Hadrian had set up prophets of the Antinous cult (also recorded in the *Historia Augusta, Life of Hadrian* 14.7).

Lucian of Samosata describes the very popular second-century oracle of Alexander and his talking snake, Glycon (a manifestation of the god Aesclepius), which operated in Abonuteichos, on the southern coast of the Black Sea.[13] Lucian, whose account is decidedly biased, mocks the many gullible from all walks of life who visited the oracle (*Alexander* 17, 30), and the cult is mentioned by Christian authors. The wide popularity, and long life, of this oracle has been well-established. Evidence includes statuettes, inscriptions, gems, and coins.[14] This oracle operated by means of sealed written inquires and also by direct, verbal responses ostensibly from the snake-god, Aesclepius-Glycon. Here is Lucian's description of its operation:

> Alexander announced to all comers that the god would make prophecies, and named a date for it in advance. He directed everyone to write down in a scroll whatever he wanted and what he especially wished to learn, to tie it up, and to seal it with wax or clay or something else of that sort. Then he himself, after taking the scrolls and entering the inner sanctuary – for

> by that time the temple had been erected and the stage set – proposed to summon in order, with herald and priest, those who had submitted them, and after the god told him about each case, to give back the scroll with the seal upon it, just as it was, and the reply to it endorsed upon it; for the god would reply explicitly to any question that anyone should put. As a matter of fact, this trick, to a man like you, and if it is not out of place to say so, like myself also, was obvious and easy to see through, but to those drivelling idiots it was miraculous and almost as good as incredible. Having discovered various ways of undoing the seals, he would read all the questions and answer them as he thought best. Then he would roll up the scrolls again, seal them, and give them back, to the great astonishment of the recipients, among whom the comment was frequent: "Why, how did he learn the questions which I gave him very securely sealed with impressions hard to counterfeit, unless there was really some god that knew everything?" . . . Again and again, as I said before, he exhibited the serpent to all who requested it, not in its entirety, but exposing chiefly the tail and the rest of the body and keeping the head out of sight under his arm. But as he wished to astonish the crowd still more, he promised to produce the god talking – delivering oracles in person without a prophet. It was no difficult matter for him to fasten cranes' windpipes together and pass them through the head, which he had so fashioned as to be lifelike. Then he answered the questions through someone else, who spoke into the tube from the outside, so that the voice issued from his canvas Asclepius.
>
> (Lucian, *Alexander* 19–20; 26)[15]

Strabo's *Geography* provides yet more oracles: the oracle of Menestheus in Iberia (3.1.9); the oracle of Fortune at Praeneste (5.3.11); the oracle of Phrixus in Moschian country (11.2.17); and one in Cilicia for Sarpedonian Artemis (14.5.19);[16] and possibly though not certainly still active, in Grynium an oracle of Apollo (13.3.5; Pausanias 1.21.7).[17]

Artemidorus, a second-century CE Greek, wrote a treatise called *The Interpretation of Dreams*. In describing dreams and their interpretation, he mentions other types of divination: physiognomists, necromancy, divining by dice, by cheese, sieves, forms, figures, palms, and dishes (2.69). The Greek magical papyri (*Papyri Graecae Magicae*, or *PGM*), is a collection of spells and rituals to control supernatural forces dating from the second century BCE to the fifth century CE. The papyri were collected in the modern age and published in a series. These spells contain many references to different types of divination using vessels of various sorts. There are divination techniques involving a bowl (3.275–81), a saucer (4.3209–54), or a lamp (4.930–1114); a boy is also often used as a medium: "Put an iron lampstand in a clean house . . . the boy should be uncorrupt, pure . . . [M]ake this boy fall into a trance and see the gods/all you are present at the divination" (*PGM* 7.540–78).[18]

Active pagan prophets are occasionally mentioned in the literary sources; Plutarch mentions a man who prophesied once a year near the Red Sea (*On the Obsolescence of Oracles* 421B); a Phrygian slave girl named Sambathis operated in Asia Minor;[19] Eunapius records the life of a female farm girl turned prophetess-philosopher, Sosipatra (Eunapius, *Lives of the Philosophers* 466–67). The Greek philosopher and wonder-worker Apollonius of Tyana was also described as a prophetic individual (*Life of Apollonius* 1.1–2; 1.32.2; 5.12; 6.3; 6.5.2–3; 7.11.3; 7.18; 7.20).

Divination might also occur through (inspired or fated) selections of texts. This was done with the *Oracles of Astrampsychus* (*Sortes Astrampsychi*) by the third century BCE (predetermined questions and answers); later there was divination via the random selection of texts of Homer and Virgil; in Christian circles, via the Bible and a text known as the *Gospel of the Lots of Mary*.[20]

This last brings us to another aspect of divination in the Empire, and that is the number of writings about divination that were produced in the imperial period. Cicero situates his own lengthy work, *On Divination*, within a long tradition of Greco-Roman writings on this topic.

> Then came Chrysippus, [third century BCE] a man of the keenest intellect, who exhaustively discussed the whole theory of divination in two books, and, besides, wrote one book on oracles and another on dreams. And following him, his pupil, Diogenes of Babylon, published one book, Antipater two, and my friend, Posidonius, five.
>
> (Cicero, *On Divination* 1.3)

In addition to *On Divination*, Cicero also wrote another work on augury alone. Appius Claudius Pulcher, the consul of 54 BCE, did as well (*On Divination* 1.47).[21] Caecina in the time of Julius Caesar wrote on the Etruscan art of divination (Pliny, *Natural History* 2.113), as did Nigidius Figulus (Pliny, *Natural History* 2.113). He was a friend of Cicero and a scholar with a particular interest in religion and divination. He produced works on augury (*Private Augury*, Aulus Gellius, *Attic Nights* 7.6.10), and on the interpretation of dreams (Servius, *On Vergil's Aeneid* 10.175). He himself was prophetic, foretelling a great future for a young Octavian (Suetonius, *Life of Augustus* 92).

In the second-century, Plutarch and Lucian produced writings on oracles. Oenomaus, a second century CE Cynic from Gadara in Transjordania, wrote a work attacking oracles. Artemidorus and Aristides wrote about dreams. In the third century, Cornelius Labeo wrote *On the Oracle of Apollo of Claros* (Aulus Gellius, *Attic Nights* 3.3.15). Neoplatonists and Theurgists of the third century produced a spate of writings on oracles and dreams, including works by Julian the Chaldean, Porphyry, and his pupil Iamblichus.[22] It is likely that there were others, but this list alone indicates an interest in divination that is easily as strong as that of the Jews or the Christians of the imperial period.

Cicero's *On Divination* is a useful work for getting a handle on the range of Greco-Roman beliefs about divination and attitudes toward it. This work is arranged as a dialogue which genre had its roots in the dialectical discussions between Socrates and his pupils (or at least in Plato's version of Socrates), in which for each issue every side is presented and all possible arguments examined from every angle. In the ancient dialogue, although its form and purpose did change over time with later, Christian dialogues becoming increasingly one-sided, Cicero seems to have chosen the dialogue form, not in order to persuade the reader to endorse one view or the other, but rather to lay them out in full. The arguments supporting divination are presented as well as arguments against it. The views espoused by each participant in a dialogue are not necessarily his own. Cicero himself, though taking up the con position, served as an augur. His brother Quintus was given the job of presenting the pro arguments. In Book 1, he does this primarily by presenting the views of the Stoic Posidonius. Stoics were well-known to believe in the reality and efficacy of divination. Cicero's arguments in Book 2 are taken from the arguments of Carneades, the second-century BCE leader of the philosophical group, the Academy, and his successor, Clitomachus of the New Academy. These were skeptics and in particular Carneades was an opponent of the Stoics. Earlier we saw how Cicero divided divination up into two categories, those which were acquired by skill and that type which occurred naturally, as the inspiration of the gods (1.18). This was a widespread categorization that we see from the time of Plato.

Cicero was a Roman, native-born, and his brother Quintus was as well. If we look elsewhere in the Empire, we can see opposing attitudes among Greek authors. Dio Chrysostom's *Orations* are peppered with negative comments on him we can compare Lucian who, although he derided the Alexander-Glycon cult in particular, thought that oracles as a whole were altogether phony (*Alexander the False Prophet*; *The Liar* 38; *Zeus the Tragic Actor* 6; 28 and 30–31; *Demonax* 37; *Dialogues of the Dead*; *Dialogues of the Gods*; *The*

Ass 37–38). Oenomaus, the second-century CE Cynic mentioned earlier, wrote a work attacking oracles; he said he had received the same reply as another client and in his work he went through examples from Greek literature to show that the oracles were not real and that Apollo was a sophist (Eusebius, *Preparation for the Gospel* 5.18–19). Plutarch, our Delphic priest, forms a strong contrast to these.

To this point, this chapter has established the prevalence of divination in the pagan Roman Empire. Greco-Roman pagans visited divination practitioners, and wrote extensively about prophecy and oracles. We turn now to the relationship between divination and the Roman state. This will form a necessary backdrop to our discussion of third-century pagan-Christian conflict below.

A number of Roman officials were tasked with consulting the gods through divination. These individuals seem to be taken from the elite class.[23] The three major priestly colleges were the pontiffs (in charge of religious customs, proper rites, and sacred law); the augurs (who divined whether the actions about to be taken had divine approval); and the *quindecemviri* (board of fifteen men who maintained and consulted the official state collection of Sibylline prophecies).[24] Out of the three main colleges then, two of them were primarily concerned with divination. *Haruspices* formed another priestly college that was in charge of divining the will of the gods, though in contrast to the augurs, who studied the flight patterns of birds, lightning and thunder, they consulted the entrails of sacrificed animals. *Haruspices* were primarily in charge of responding to prodigies though the college of the *quindecemviri* might be said to overlap with them in this respect. Valerius Maximus, a first-century author who had investigated and written about Roman religion, describes the importance of divination to the foundation of the Roman state:

> Our ancestors decreed that fixed and customary ceremonies be managed through the science of Pontiffs, guidance for the good conduct of affairs through the observations of Augurs, Apollo's prophecies through books of the seers, aversion of portents through Etruscan discipline. By ancient ordinance also rituals are performed: in commending, by prayer; in demanding, by vow; in discharging, by offer of thanks; in enquiring, whether by entrails or lots, by solicitation of response; in performing of customary rite, by sacrifice, wherewith also warnings of prodigies or lightnings are expiated.
>
> (*Memorable Deeds and Sayings* 1.1)

There were nineteen augurs under Augustus (the number of which had increased over time).[25] Taking the auspices referred to the consultation of the will of the gods for any important undertaking, be it political or military. Cicero writes,

> Romulus, the father of this City, not only founded it in obedience to the auspices, but was himself a most skillful augur. Next, the other Roman kings employed augurs; and, again, after the expulsion of the kings, no public business was ever transacted at home or abroad without first taking the auspices.
> (*On Divination* 1.2)

Auspices could be taken by observing things that happened in specially designated spaces in the sky.[26] This might be by observing the flight of birds, or by observing the pattern of lightning or thunder. The auspices could also be taken by observing the actions of animals. The state had consecrated poultry or sacred chickens and their eating habits could also be consulted (see Livy 10.40.1 and Cicero, *On Divination* 1.15 and 2.34–35). The augurs did not observe entrails or prodigies. For many rites, there were two necessary participants which Scheid defines as active and passive; this could be two religious officials such as a pontiff and a flamen or it could be a magistrate (active) and an augur (passive).[27] What made rites effective was to perform correctly the correct rite for the occasion.[28] When augurs were elected for office they had no prior training, but the appointment was for life and they would learn on the job. The records of their predecessors were available for consultation (on the appointment of augurs for life, see Pliny the Younger, *Letters* 4.8 and Plutarch, *Roman Questions*).[29] Their job was to be present as a witness when a magistrate did the auspices; the college would be tasked with delivering judgment on whether the proceedings were legal or not.[30] They were also in charge of inaugurations and of demarcating and defining sacred space.[31]

Haruspices interpreted prodigies. The term prodigy refers to any unusual occurrence such as a natural disaster or unusual birth. It was an indication that something was wrong and the gods needed to be consulted.[32] *Haruspicy* had begun as a foreign, Etruscan science, but there was an official Roman college by the end of the Republic, which was consulted by the Senate (Livy 22.1.8–20; 43.13; for an illustrating example of interaction between the Senate and the college, see Cicero's *Response to the Haruspices* 5.9 and 6.11).[33] The form of divination practiced by the *haruspices* involved the examination of the entrails of sacrificed animals, in particular the livers. It was believed that the gods sculpted the shape of the livers, and certain configurations were associated with favorable or unfavorable messages (see Cicero, *On Divination* 1.52 for a description and Aeschylus, *Prometheus Bound* 484–99). At sacrifices, the *haruspices* would inspect the victims' livers to make sure that there were no unfavorable signs – that the sacrifice was a "go," in other words (Livy 41.14–16). The governors' staffs included them as did the army.[34]

The college of the *quindecemviri* was in charge of the Sibylline Books. Other duties (which may be related to these) followed including being in charge of the great celebration, the *Ludi Saeculares* (Secular Games, which were established on the basis of the Books); being a priest of the Magna Mater (the Great Mother, also introduced to Rome through consultation of the Books) and serving as priests of Apollo (with whom the Sibyl and prophecy in general were associated).[35] The state's Sibylline Books (*Libri Sibyllini*) are to be differentiated from the Jewish and Christian Sibylline Oracles (*Oracula Sibyllina*). They were believed to be from the Sibyl at Cumae, in Greece, and to have been purchased for the state by the elder King Tarquinius (Dionysius of Halicarnassus 4.62.1–4). The college was in charge of the Books and would be asked to consult them when there was uncertainty: defeat in war, the misconduct of a Vestal Virgin, the birth of a hermaphrodite. The college would consult the books and report to the Senate what they had to say about the current situation. The Senate would then decide what action to take. Often the response was cult-centered: the gods required the performance of particular rites or the introduction of a new cult. The extant sources quote only one oracle; all of the other literary references from antiquity merely describe what prompted the consultation and the action taken in response.

> In short, there is no possession of the Romans, sacred or profane, which they guard so carefully as they do the Sibylline oracles. They consult them, by order of the senate, when the state is in the grip of party strife or some great misfortune has happened to them in war, or some important prodigies and apparitions have been seen which are difficult of interpretation, as has often happened.
>
> (Dionysius of Halicarnassus 4.62.5)

From the evidence that we do have, we can see that the Romans consulted the Books regularly over the course of the Republic. But the credible sources for the imperial period record only a few instances of consultation. Augustus and Tiberius both ordered an inventory and sifting of the books (Suetonius, *Life of Augustus* 31; Cassius Dio 54.17.2; Tacitus, *Annals* 6.2; discussed below). Augustus used their contents to legitimize his establishment of a set of spectacular games, the *Ludi Saeculares* in 17 BCE.[36] Claudius later re-interpreted the chronology of this oracle so that he too, might hold the games (Tacitus,

Annals 11.15). Nero intervened to stop the panic that was induced by an ominous, popular interpretation of an oracle (Cassius Dio 62.18.3–4; discussed below).

These were the state-supported forms of divination. As for private practitioners, the state had a complicated relationship with this group.[37] There were three main ways that the imperial center interacted with prophets who were not appointed by the Roman state: (1) the state attempted to control dangerous elements; (2) prophets and prophecy were used to legitimize, to set the seal of divine approval, on emperors or imperial pretenders; and (3) emperors interacted with prophets and oracles in their role as supporters and arbiters of traditional religion.

Divination of any type always had the potential to be subversive. Even state-sanctioned diviners were appealing to a higher authority than that of the emperor. Celts, Jews, and Egyptians were three groups who had a long tradition of native prophets who sometimes dabbled in nationalistic prophecies (for Gauls and Germans see Tacitus, *Germania* 10; Tacitus, *Histories* 4.54).[38] These groups were put down through military force.

The emperors occasionally produced bans against private, individual practitioners. Emperors did not want to see their subjects in direct contact with the divine and therefore wanted to control access to the divine but could never be totally successful. We mentioned earlier several active pagan prophets, and the *PGM* also indicates that there were a goodly number of diviners practicing without hindrance.

Overall, the legislation against divination is piecemeal, directed against particular groups or specific practices.[39] For example, Augustus forbade prophets to prophesy to one individual alone or for prophets to prophesy about a death (Cassius Dio 56.25.5). Astrology was considered to be particularly dangerous as it opened up an avenue for speculation as to the fate of the emperor. Claudius, like several other emperors, banned astrologers from Italy (Cassius Dio 61.33) but also one individual in particular: "Furius Scribonianus was driven into exile, on a charge of inquiring into the end of the sovereign by the agency of astrologers" (Tacitus, *Annals* 12.52.1). Astrologers urged Otho to attempt a coup (Tacitus, *Histories* 1.22), and astrologers posted anti-Vitellius messages in the city (Suetonius, *Life of Vitellius* 14.4). Vespasian banned them from Rome (Cassius Dio 65.9.2). Hadrian, according to a late source, blocked up a prophetic spring from which he had obtained a prophecy of his future emperorship. The emperor did not want anyone else to be able to be able to repeat the experience (Ammianus Marcellinus 22.12.8; Sozomen, *Church*

History 5.19). Severus had his stars painted on the ceilings of his palace, but was careful to have two versions painted, so as to conceal his fate from others (Cassius Dio 77.11.1–2).

But even against the astrologers, the emperors never held out for long, as we see in this episode from the life of the emperor Tiberius:

> But as for all the other astrologers and magicians and such as practised divination in any other way whatsoever, he put to death those who were foreigners and banished all the citizens that were accused of still employing the art at this time after the previous decree by which it had been forbidden to engage in any such business in the city; but to those that obeyed immunity was granted. In fact, all the citizens would have been acquitted even contrary to his wish, had not a certain tribune prevented it.
>
> (Cassius Dio 57.15.8; compare Suetonius, *Life of Tiberius* 36 and 63)

Augustus, that master of public relations, in a reversal from the norm, celebrated his good fortune publicly.

> While in retirement at Apollonia, Augustus mounted with Agrippa to the studio of the astrologer Theogenes. Agrippa was the first to try his fortune, and when a great and almost incredible career was predicted for him, Augustus persisted in concealing the time of his birth and in refusing to disclose it, through diffidence and fear that he might be found to be less eminent. When he at last gave it unwillingly and hesitatingly, and only after many requests, Theogenes sprang up and threw himself at his feet. From that time on Augustus had such faith in his destiny, that he made his horoscope public and issued a silver coin stamped with the sign of the constellation Capricornus, under which he was born.
>
> (Suetonius, *Life of Augustus* 94.12)

In this case, Augustus' horoscope confirmed that he had divine sanction to rule. This explains why the emperors were not consistently strict when it came to unofficial divination; they could not afford to do without prophecy altogether because it was a part of the imperial legitimation process. An excellent example of this can be seen in Suetonius, *Life of Augustus* 92–95, already cited, or in the similar record of prophetic proofs in the biography of Vespasian. Suetonius provides us with a full description of the many signs and favorable prophecies that preceded Vespasian's reign (Suetonius, *Life of Vespasian* 5). Some of these, like that of Josephus, were made spontaneously (Josephus, *Jewish War*

3.399–407); others were sought out by Vespasian himself (for his consultation of the god at Alexandria, see Tacitus, *Histories* 4.82). In the imperial biographies, whether the emperors were portrayed as good emperors or bad emperors, successful or short-lived, prophecies were made about them and they were themselves described as seeking guidance as to whether or not they should try to rule or how they would rule. There are enough variations among these biographical accounts and enough parallels with other sources to argue against seeing this connection between emperors and prophets as a literary trope.[40]

Beginning with Augustus, Roman emperors assumed responsibility for the oversight of traditional religion, both in Rome and in the provinces.[41] In Cassius Dio's history of Augustus, Maecenas lays out a blueprint for the imperial relationship to the gods of Rome and the gods of the Empire.

> Therefore, if you desire to become in very truth immortal, act as I advise; and, furthermore, do you not only yourself worship the divine Power everywhere and in every way in accordance with the traditions of our fathers, but compel all others to honour it. Those who attempt to distort our religion with strange rites you should abhor and punish, not merely for the sake of the gods (since if a man despises these he will not pay honour to any other being), but because such men, by bringing in new divinities in place of the old, persuade many to adopt foreign practices, from which spring up conspiracies, factions, and cabals, which are far from profitable to a monarchy. Do not, therefore, permit anybody to be an atheist or a sorcerer. Soothsaying, to be sure, is a necessary art, and you should by all means appoint some men to be diviners and augurs, to whom those will resort who wish to consult them on any matter; that there ought to be no workers in magic at all. For such men, by speaking the truth sometimes, but generally falsehood, often encourage a great many to attempt revolutions.
>
> (52.36.1–3)

Emperors were expected to provide support for traditional religion and as we would expect, we do see imperial patronage of pagan oracles. *Asylia* was granted for the sanctuary at Miletus in 22 CE, which would include the Didyma oracle (Tacitus, *Annals* 2.63). Caligula, Trajan, Hadrian, Diocletian, and Maximian gave imperial benefactions of buildings, processional pathways, and statues to Didyma (Suetonius, *Life of Caligula* 21; Cassius Dio 59.28). Trajan and Hadrian were both given the honorary titles of "prophet" there. Hadrian was also a benefactor of the oracle at Claros. He completed or financed the grand temple of Apollo in that complex.[42]

Emperors were in charge of protecting right relations with the gods, and this could include intervening to settle matters relating to prophetic interpretation that pertained to the Empire. Augustus, for example, acted to preserve accurate copies of the Sibylline Books, as did other emperors. He had 2,000 books of faux-prophecy burned:

> [He] collected whatever prophetic writings of Greek or Latin origin were in circulation anonymously or under the names of authors of little repute, and burned more than two thousand of them, retaining only the Sibylline books and making a choice even among those; and he deposited them in two gilded cases under the pedestal of the Palatine Apollo.
>
> (Suetonius, *Life of Augustus* 31.1)

Augustus also had the books copied out by the priests "with their own hands" in order that no unauthorized persons might see them (Cassius Dio 54.17.2). In Tiberius' reign, there were two attempts on the part of officials to introduce the Books into public life. In the first instance, recorded in Tacitus, *Annals* 1.76, the Tiber had flooded and destroyed parts of the city (15 CE). Asinius Gallus proposed that the Books be consulted. Tiberius refused the request and assigned two men to tackle the matter. Later in his reign, in 32 CE, a member of the *quindecemvirate*, operating in conjunction with the plebian tribune, tried to push through the Senate a proposal to recognize as authentic additional Sibylline oracles. Tiberius intervened: many oracles were in circulation under the name of the Sibyl, and it was for the experts in the college to carefully sift through them and determine which were authentic. Tiberius called upon imperial precedent, noting that Augustus had already outlawed private possession of the oracles (Tacitus, *Annals* 6.12).

Unauthorized Sibylline oracles seem to have been a problem in the imperial age. The first Books had been destroyed by fire in the second century BCE, and the entire collection had to be replaced. Dionysius of Halicarnassus records that after the original Books were destroyed by a fire, the state sent out a delegation to find "authentic" oracles (Dionysius of Halicarnassus 4.62.6). In Cassius Dio 57.18.3–4, in the year 19 CE, Tiberius is described as intervening to calm popular unease caused by a number of signs appearing suddenly in conjunction with the circulation of an ominous, unauthorized oracle. Dio writes:

> They were furthermore disturbed not a little by an oracle, reputed to be an utterance of the Sibyl, which, although it did not fit this period of the city's history at all, was nevertheless applied to the situation then existing. It ran: "When thrice three hundred revolving years have run their course, Civil strife upon Rome destruction shall bring, and the folly, too, Of Sybaris . . ." Tiberius, now, denounced these verses as spurious and made an investigation of all the books that contained any prophecies, rejecting some as worthless and retaining others as genuine.

Under Nero this oracle would again be brought forward after the Great Fire of 64 CE (Cassius Dio 62.18.3). Nero reassured the populace that this one was a fake – it was not found in the official Books. But they merely dredged up another:

> And when Nero, by way of encouraging them, reported that these verses could not be found anywhere, they dropped them and proceeded to repeat another oracle, which they averred to be a genuine Sibylline prophecy, namely: "Last of the sons of Aeneas, a mother-slayer shall govern." And so it proved, whether this verse was actually spoken beforehand by some divine prophecy, or the populace was now for the first time inspired, in view of the present situation, to utter it.
>
> (Cassius Dio 62.18.4)

The Roman state during the Empire had a strong relationship with both official and unofficial divination. Divination was part of the apparatus of Empire; the state regularly performed rites of divination as part of its daily operations and it maintained a collection of special prophetic oracles. Emperors consulted oracles and prophets and emperors supported oracular centers. Emperors sometimes acted to restrain prophetic activity or texts that were causing popular disturbances but in the main allowed it and them to exist unhindered.

Sources for the third century indicate a high level of activity at pagan oracles and a deep engagement with divination and with oracles in particular in pagan religious discourse. We have already mentioned above the flourishing of oracles that occurred at this time. Also mentioned was the third-century work of Cornelius Labeo, *On the Oracle of Apollo of Claros*, no longer extant.

We turn now to those pagan texts from the third century CE about prophets, prophecy, and oracles that have survived.

The literature and teachings associated with Hermes Trismegistus played a prominent part in pagan discourse about prophecy and oracles in the third century CE. Hermes was associated with an Egyptian god, Thoth, but his teachings were taken up by Greek philosophers as well as by Gnostics and orthodox Christians. He was called thrice-great (Trismegistus), and was the deity in charge of healing and learning. He was also a heavenly scribe, recording the deeds of humankind for judgment, and he was associated with revealing the divine to humans. It is in this last function that his connection to revelatory, prophetic writings developed. Christian authors appropriated his teachings in a way similar to those of the Sibyl, to prove that divinely inspired pagans agreed with Christian teaching (Lactantius, *Divine Institutes* 1.6; 4.6–8; 7.18).

The main Hermetic corpus as we have it today consists of eighteen Greek treatises which were brought together over time into one collection, although they were originally produced in various times and places. There were also three Hermetic Coptic texts in the Nag Hammadi codices, and a Latin work, *Asclepius*, which was completed by the third century CE; the last major source is an anthology composed around 500 CE. The last two overlap to some extent with earlier materials but also contain some material not found elsewhere.[43] Although we may not be able to precisely date each of these texts, we can be reasonably confident that this type of material was circulating in the third century CE.

One of the Hermetic texts from the Nag Hammadi codices, *The Perfect Discourse*, contains a prediction of future woes to Egypt which was to be followed by a restoration (70.3–74.17).[44] This text includes a section on the judgment of souls and the punishment of the wicked (76.19–78.31). This text has obvious parallels with Gnostic literature, and with Judeo-Christian apocalyptic literature. Another Hermetic text, *Corpus Hermeticum* 1, also has parallels to Judeo-Christian revelation literature. In this text, Hermes Trismegistus sees a vision of everything which is brought to him by Poimandres, the Mind of Sovereignty. This text ends with Hermes Trismegistus trying to share his message on earth and, like a prophet from the Jewish Scriptures, being rejected by some (27–29). In *Corpus Hermeticum* 11, the Mind discloses to Hermes the truth about the God and the universe, including the cosmos, and the seven worlds below, though the description of the latter is quite brief and summary. The ideas expressed in Iamblichus, another third-century pagan author who we will take up below, on the ascent of the pure soul and union with the divine are echoed in the *Discourse on the Eighth and Ninth* (see especially 56–57), another Hermetic text found at Nag Hammadi. Iamblichus specifically mentions Hermetic teaching as a source of true knowledge at a number of places in his *On the Mysteries* (1.2; 8.1–6).

But Hermes Trismegistus was associated with texts dealing with a wide range of subjects, including healing, magic, astrology, and alchemy, and it is difficult to piece together a coherent, systematic Hermetic theology. We cannot use Iamblichus to reconstruct the Hermetic ideas he was incorporating; it is possible that he was merely appropriating the "label" of Hermetic teaching for his own brand of Neoplatonic, theurgistic theology. It is safest to consider the Hermetic corpus as an amorphous collection of texts and teachings, one that could absorb and reflect the sorts of philosophical and religious teaching that we also see among the Neoplatonists and theurgists, like Porphyry and Iamblichus, that we will take up next, although it may have included other things in addition to these.

Iamblichus and Porphyry were third-century pagans who both wrote extensively on prophecy and oracles. They were in dialogue with earlier philosophers and religious figures, with Christians, and with each other, so they may serve as good examples of the types of ideas floating around in pagan circles in the Roman Empire in the third century CE. Topics which they discuss in their writings included the traditional elements of religion, ritual, cult statues, sacrifices, daemons, the parts of the soul, healing, fate, dreams, how divine inspiration worked, and theurgy.

Crystal Addey has written about Iamblichus and Porphyry in her book *Divination and Theurgy in Neoplatonism*: *Oracles of the Gods*. Porphyry and Iamblichus were both Neoplatonists, and Iamblichus was also what is known as a theurgist. Addey defines theurgy (*theourgia*) as "god-working" or "divine work." In her reconstruction, which is largely followed here, the founder of the theurgy movement was one Julian the Chaldean. This man was credited with inventing the term theurgy, and he, along with his son, Julian the Theurgist, was the author of the second-third century text, the *Chaldean Oracles*.[45] This work, which is extant now only in fragments, consisted of short oracular statements about cosmology, metaphysics, ethics, and ritual.[46] Porphyry wrote a commentary on the *Chaldean Oracles*. He and Iamblichus both take up the ideas presented in the Chaldean teachings.

Iamblichus' *On the Mysteries* was a reply to Porphyry's *Letter to Anebo* written about 280–305 CE. The two works have long been interpreted as illustrating a disagreement between the two men over the place of ritual in achieving unity with the divine, but Addey has shown through her analysis of these texts that Iamblichus and Porphyry were rather engaging in a traditional dialogue in which all sides of an issue were to be explored in full.[47]

In Iamblichus, *On the Mysteries* Book 3, he takes up the origins of divination. He endeavors to explain its ultimate and penultimate origins, and he discusses at great length the many factors that he believes impact divination. Although the lesser gods are said to inspire divination, the One God is ultimately the source for all true divination. Divine inspiration is everywhere, permeating everything (1.9). What prohibits humans from fully knowing the will of the gods at all times, from being able to connect to the divine completely and properly, is a lack of proper purification and the presence of complicating, interfering factors.

Iamblichus has two categories of divination, which Addey terms the inspired and the inductive, and these are placed in a hierarchy which is based on "proximity to divinity."[48] Divination by induction, or technique, is the lesser sort. This type involves some level of human skill or human intuition. This type also has it root origins in the One God but because it is mediated through nature, good or bad daemons, and through humans, it is necessarily inferior, able only to predict non-consequential things (3.5, 7, 15–16, 26; 6.4; 10.3–5).[49]

False divination is created when complicating factors intervene such as an evil daemon, or a soul that is distracted (3.7, 13, 31). The One God will communicate fully only with the pure soul. To the degree that humans are purified enough, they will receive prophetic power (3.31). This purity is achieved through theurgistic practice (10.5–6).

For Iamblichus, divination inspiration is important to theurgic ritual (3.31).[50] As Addey puts it, for theurgists, the goal of divination was not so much prophecies about the future or information about the will of the divine but rather union with it. According to Iamblichus, through divination, the theurgist would ascend and connect to the divine. He would become one with the deity and therefore be able to speak in the language of the gods, pronouncing his own oracles.[51]

> This, then, is one kind of mantic, which is undefiled and sacerdotal, and truly divine . . . And it is proper for you and everyone who is a genuine lover of the gods to surrender himself to it wholly. For in such a fashion arises, at the same time, both infallible truth in oracles, and perfect virtue in souls. With both of these, ascent to the intelligible fire is granted to the theurgists, a process which indeed must be proposed as the goal of all foreknowledge and of every theurgic operation.
>
> (3.31)[52]

Porphyry (who lived approximately 234–305 CE) was writing in the latter part of the third and very early fourth centuries. He collected oracles in three books which seem to come primarily from his own time and which included oracles from Delphi, Didyma, and Claros. Porphyry also wrote on astrology and wrote several treatises against the Christians.[53] The relationship between his writings against Christians and his major work on oracles is unclear: these may in fact be parts of the same text; alternatively, he may have repeated material from the one in the other. Surviving references to his writings against the Christians do not allow us to determine definitively whether there was one discrete text with this title. His *Philosophy from Oracles* is preserved in forty-eight fragments, most of which can be found in Eusebius and Augustine, and this is the work that will be predominantly taken up in what follows, though we begin with an examination of his dialogue with Iamblichus as found in Porphyry's *Letter to Anebo* and Iamblichus' *On the Mysteries*.[54]

Porphyry in the *Letter to Anebo* challenges Iamblichus to defend his philosophical and religious ideas, including his beliefs about theurgy and divination. Porphyry asks how divination works, and he provides an overview of current beliefs about divination, including beliefs of the theurgists. Taking all of his writings together as a whole, it is not quite clear what Porphyry's stance on theurgy was. It is thought, based on Augustine's depiction of him, that Porphyry was anti-ritual or perhaps thought that ritual was effective only as a tool of purification for the "lower soul" but that the "intellectual soul" could achieve full unity with the divine without any sort of materiality.[55] Yet he did write a commentary on the *Chaldean Oracles*, which he himself was the first to bring into Neoplatonism, and from his fragmentary writings we can identify areas of correspondence to Iamblichus with respect to divination.

Areas of overlap with Iamblichus include:[56]

1. The gods themselves desire to have cult statues and tell humans how to construct these; the implication is that these statues serve as conduits to the gods (Iamblichus, *On the Mysteries* 5.23; Eusebius, *Preparation for the Gospel* 5.12–15).[57]
2. The sympathy principle: this refers to the great chain of being, the divine force that permeates all of the cosmos (Eusebius, *Preparation for the Gospel* 4.9; Iamblichus, *On the Mysteries* 3.16; 4.9–10; 5.20).[58]
3. False divination arises from intervening factors (Eusebius, *Preparation for the Gospel* 6.5; Iamblichus, *On the Mysteries* 3.7, 13, 31).

4 There is a link between true, accurate divination and purification of the soul (Eusebius, *Preparation for the Gospel* 4.7; Iamblichus, *On the Mysteries* 3.31).
5 A refutation of Christian teachings about pagan oracles (Iamblichus, *On the Mysteries* 3.31; for Porphyry, see below).

In respect to this last point, although the *Letter of Anebo* presents the Christian belief that pagan divination was the product of daemons, Porphyry is not giving us his own point of view in this text. For Porphyry's own beliefs about oracles, we must rely on the fragments of his *Of the Philosophy to be derived from Oracles* and to other scattered references among his extant fragments (not all of which we can match to a specific text) to prophecy and the interpretation of prophetic texts among the Christian community. It is here that Porphyry's strong, negative opinions about the ways in which Christians interacted with prophecy and prophetic texts are expressed. We will turn now to an examination of Porphyry's writings about prophecy, prophets, and oracles, and to the fierce response that this produced among Christians.

Eusebius tells us what Porphyry's aim was:

> He therefore, in the book which he entitled *Of the Philosophy to be derived from Oracles*, made a collection of the oracles of Apollo and the other gods and good daemons, which he especially chose out of them as thinking that they would suffice both for proof of the excellence of the supposed deities, and for the encouragement of what he is pleased to call "Theosophy."
>
> (Eusebius, *Preparation for the Gospel* 4.6)[59]

In the surviving excerpts from the work, although he objected to Christian interpretive strategies, we can see some similarities between Porphyry's approach to the pagan oracles that he transcribes and the Christian approach to the Jewish Scriptures. Of the pagan oracles, Porphyry writes,

> Sure, then, and steadfast is he who draws his hopes of salvation from this as from the only sure source . . . For I myself call the gods to witness, that I have neither added anything, nor taken away . . . so that I preserved the sense of what was spoken untouched, guarding against the impiety of such changes, rather than against the avenging justice that follows from the sacrilege.
>
> (Eusebius, *Preparation for the Gospel* 4.7)

This is reminiscent of Christian notions of a scriptural canon and using texts as a means of accessing the divine. Seeing the prophetic texts as a road to "salvation" is an idea we saw in Clement in Chapter 2; Josephus also had stated that "by all kinds of premonitory signs" God "shows His people the way of salvation" (*Jewish Wars* 6.310).

What does Porphyry think his oracle collection will do for people? What is its practical purpose?

> And our present collection will contain a record of many doctrines of philosophy, according as the gods declared the truth to be; but to a small extent we shall also touch upon the practice of divination, such as will be useful both for contemplation, and for the general purification of life. And the utility which this collection possesses will be best known to as many as have ever been in travail with the truth, and prayed that by receiving the manifestation of it from the gods they might gain relief from their perplexity by virtue of the trustworthy teaching of the speakers.
> (Eusebius, *Preparation for the Gospel* 4.7)

Like the Christian Scriptures, the pagan oracles are to be consulted for use in daily life, for navigating one's day-to-day experiences and providing hope and comfort. Porphyry also explicates the theology behind the oracles in a manner similar to that of the Christian biblical exegetes. Like Tertullian, who wrote of the different layers of meaning to be taken from the Scripture, Porphyry sees a deeper, non-literal sense behind the words of the oracles in his collection.

> Next in order after what has been said concerning piety we shall record the responses given by them concerning their worship, part of which by anticipation we have set forth in the statements concerning piety. Now this is the response of Apollo, containing at the same time an orderly classification of the gods. . . .

Then a few words later he [Porphyry] explains this response, interpreting it as follows:

> Now this is the method of the sacrifices, which are rendered according to the aforesaid classification of the gods. For whereas there are gods beneath the earth, and on the earth, and those beneath the earth are called also infernal gods, and those on the earth terrestrial, for all these in common he enjoins the sacrifice of black four-footed victims. But with regard

> to the manner of the sacrifice he makes a difference: for to terrestrial gods he commands the victims to be slain upon altars, but to the infernal gods over trenches, and moreover after the offering to bury the bodies therein.
> (Eusebius, *Preparation for the Gospel* 4.9)

For Porphyry, the oracles, like the Christian Scriptures, could be read allegorically and like them or other Christian visionary writings, they provided information about the cosmos and the gods.

Chapter 2 mentioned that several early church fathers discuss the proper way to read Scripture. Origen in particular was considered to be an allegorist extraordinaire. Gregory Thaumaturgos, writing in approximately 238 CE, praised him for his skills, describing his abilities as an interpreter of the prophets, which, to his mind, must have been bestowed by heaven itself (*Oration and Panegyric Addressed to Origen* 15). Here again, then, is our inspired interpreter, such as we saw in Second Temple Judaism. As is discussed in a 2005 publication by Robert Berchman, Porphyry, who it should be noted singled out Origen for special condemnation, thought that the Christians were wrong to interpret their Scriptures allegorically; the subject matter, the Jewish Scriptures themselves, were too simple a material to warrant the application of complex interpretive strategies.[60] According to Porphyry, Christians only applied allegory to their sacred writings in order to explain away inconsistencies in the texts in an illegitimate way (Eusebius, *Church History* 6.4).[61]

Porphyry had studied the Jewish Scriptures (Theodoret of Cyrrhus, *Therapeia of the Greek Maladies* 7; fifth century CE) and attacked the Christian interpretation of them with vigor. In particular, Porphyry went after the Book of Daniel because he realized that it was central to the Christian view of Christ and the Christian view of history.[62] Porphyry aimed to show that Daniel did not represent true prophecy but was rather a pseudepigraphic writing, a fake, self-consciously crafted to pose as a real prophecy. He brought forward evidence to prove that the book had been produced in the time of Antiochus Epiphanes IV and was thus a present-day author speaking about the past and contemporary events, rather than a person writing in the far past about the events of the future. Jerome in the prologue to his *Commentary on Daniel* sums up Porphyry's main line of attack:

> Porphyry wrote his twelfth book against the prophecy of Daniel, denying that it was composed by the person to whom it is ascribed in its title, but rather by some individual living in Judaea at the time of the Antiochus who was surnamed Epiphanes. He furthermore alleged that "Daniel" did

> not foretell the future so much as he related the past, and lastly that whatever he spoke of up till the time of Antiochus contained authentic history, whereas anything he may have conjectured beyond that point was false, inasmuch as he would not have foreknown the future.[63]

Porphyry also identified Christian misattributions of prophetic texts (Jerome, *Tractate on the Psalms* 77; Jerome, *Commentary on Matthew* 3:3). Overall, Porphyry concluded that Jesus was a wise man, but his followers had misunderstood him and had tried to make him out to be something more than he was (Augustine, *City of God* 19.23), and we can see this attitude mirrored in pagan oracles of this time period. According to Augustine (lived 354–28 August 430 CE):

> For in his book called ἐκ λογίων φιλοσοφίας, [*On the Philosophy of Oracles*] in which he collects and comments upon the responses which he pretends were uttered by the gods concerning divine things, he says – I give his own words as they have been translated from the Greek: "To one who inquired what god he should propitiate in order to recall his wife from Christianity, Apollo replied in the following verses." Then the following words are given as those of Apollo: "You will probably find it easier to write lasting characters on the water, or lightly fly like a bird through the air, than to restore right feeling in your impious wife once she has polluted herself. Let her remain as she pleases in her foolish deception, and sing false laments to her dead God, who was condemned by right-minded judges, and perished ignominiously by a violent death." Then after these verses of Apollo (which we have given in a Latin version that does not preserve the metrical form), he goes on to say: "In these verses Apollo exposed the incurable corruption of the Christians, saying that the Jews, rather than the Christians, recognized God."
>
> (Augustine, *City of God* 19.23)

Augustine is a latecomer to the acrimonious, and sometimes posthumous, debate that Christians pursued with Porphyry. Methodious of Olympus, Apollonarius of Laodicea, Lactantius, and Eusebius had preceded him. Lactantius (lived approximately 250–325 CE) directs his *Divine Institutes* in part against anti-Christian writings produced in the context of the persecution under Diocletian, including those of Porphyry (if *Divine Institutes* 5.2 does indeed refer to him).[64] He and Eusebius (lived 260/265–339/340 CE) were heavily invested in the defense of Christian prophecy over and against what they perceived as false, daemonic, pagan prophecy.

Lactantius records another anti-Christian oracular response from the oracle of Apollo at Miletus, that is the oracle at Didyma. The oracle, on being consulted as to the nature of the Christian Christ, replied: "He was mortal as to His body, being wise with wondrous works; but being taken with arms under Chaldean judges, with nails and the cross He endured a bitter end" (*Divine Institutes* 4.13). Tensions between pagans and Christians involving prophecy and oracles progress from the second century to the third century. We have already seen how Christians in the second century were appropriating the Sibylline oracles. And Celsus writing in the second half of the second century had complained of both the Christian attitude toward pagan divination and their attitude toward current, active prophets.

> Celsus goes on to say of us: They set no value on the oracles of the Pythian priestess, of the priests of Dodona, of Clarus, of Branchidae, of Jupiter Ammon, and of a multitude of others; although under their guidance we may say that colonies were sent forth, and the whole world peopled. But those sayings which were uttered or not uttered in Judea, after the manner of that country, as indeed they are still delivered among the people of Phoenicia and Palestine – these they look upon as marvellous sayings, and unchangeably true.
>
> (Origen, *Against Celsus* 7.3)

Origen (184/185–253/254 CE), though he wrote after Celsus had died, took up Celsus' objections and labored to refute him in exquisite detail point by point. Iamblichus expresses strong contempt for the Christian view that daemons were the source of pagan oracles (*On the Mysteries* 3.31). Dionysius of Alexandria, the third-century bishop of Alexandria, records the first connection between persecution and divination; in 248 CE, the outbreak of violence against the Christians that took place in that city were spurred by the fiery rhetoric of an anti-Christian, pagan prophet. Then, in 303 CE, Diocletian launched a persecution against Christians. Christian sources are clear: this was an attack by a pagan oracle on the Christians.

In Book 4 of his *Divine Institutes*, Lactantius takes up oracles and prophecies. He seeks to demonstrate that pagan oracles are both good and bad; they are wrong and daemonic when they induce belief in pagan deities, but have still been put to good use by God to point mankind in the right direction, agreeing with and pointing the way toward Christian teaching (specifically those of the Sibyl, Apollo at Colophon and Didyma, Hystaspes, and Trismegistus; see *Divine Institutes* 1.6–7; 2.9, 11, 16–17; 4.6–8, 13, 15, 17–20; 5.14; 6.25; 7.4, 7, 13, 15, 18–20, 23–25). Jewish prophetic texts, although misunderstood by the

Jews, when correctly understood also point the way toward Christ. In short, the message of the gospel was foretold in both Jewish and pagan prophecies.[65] We saw similar ideas in second-century Christian authors and see them also in the writings of Eusebius. Eusebius would respond specifically to the writings of Porphyry and launch a full-scale attack on pagan oracles.

In his works, *Preparation for the Gospel* and *Demonstration of the Gospel*, Eusebius attempts to explain the unique character of the Christian community, to explain why the Christian faith is the oldest, and best, doctrine by which to live. He explains its relationship to Judaism, and to paganism. And he devotes quite a lot of space to demonstrating that ancient Jewish prophecies prove these facts. This is clearly expressed in the opening of his *Demonstration*:

> Grant then, dear friend, my request, and labour with me henceforward in your prayers in my effort to present the Proof of the Gospel from the prophecies extant among the Hebrews from the earliest times. I propose to adopt this method. I propose to use as witnesses those men, beloved by God, whose fame you know to be far-spread in the world: Moses, I mean, and his successors, who shone forth with resplendent godliness, and the blessed prophets and sacred writers. I propose to shew, by quotations from them, how they forestalled events that came to the light long ages after their time, the actual circumstances of the Saviour's own presentment of the Gospel, and the things which in our own day are being fulfilled by the Holy Spirit before our very eyes. It shall be my task to prove that they saw that which was not present as present, and that which as yet was not in existence as actually existing; and not only this, but that they foretold in writing the events of the future for posterity, so that by their help others can even now know what is coming, and look forward daily to the fulfilment of their oracles. What sort of fulfilment, do you ask? They are fulfilled in countless and all kinds of ways, and amid all circumstances, both generally and in minute detail, in the lives of individual men, and in their corporate life, now nationally in the course of Hebrew history, and now in that of foreign nations. Such things as civic revolutions, changes of times, national vicissitudes, the coming of foretold prosperity, the assaults of adversity, the enslaving of races, the besieging of cities, the downfall and restoration of whole states, and countless other things that were to take place a long time after, were foretold by these writers.
>
> (Eusebius, *Demonstration of the Gospel* pref.)[66]

Pagan oracles come in for their fair share of attention in these works. Pagan oracles are false, daemonic, and well on their way to extinction (*Preparation for the Gospel* 2.3; 4.1–3; 5.4, 16; 6.1–5; *Demonstration of the Gospel* 5, pref.). The prophecies contained in the Jewish Scriptures foretell the coming of Christ and the Christian faith and are true (*Preparation for the Gospel* 1.1; 4.21; Books 7–15; *Demonstration of the Gospel passim*). Yet the truth of these Jewish Scriptures is sometimes reflected in pagan oracles such as the Sibyl and even those recorded by Porphyry himself (*Preparation for the Gospel* Book 9; *Demonstration of the Gospel* 3.3, 7). In the *Demonstration*, Eusebius includes an extract from the writings of Porphyry in which he recounts an oracular consultation about the nature of Christ:

> What I am about to say may seem surprising to some. It is that the gods have pronounced Christ to have been most holy and immortal, and they speak of Him reverently.

And lower down he [Porphyry] adds:

> To those asking the question, "Is Christ a God?" the oracle replied:
> "That the soul goes forth immortal after (its severance from) the body.
> Thou knowest, severed from wisdom it ever roams.
> That soul is the soul of a man signal in holiness."

He [Porphyry] certainly says here that He was most holy, and that His soul, which the Christians ignorantly worship, like the souls of others, was made immortal after death. And when asked, "Why did He suffer?" the oracle replied:

> "The body of the weak has ever been exposed to torments,
> But the soul of holy men takes its place in heaven."

And he [Porphyry] adds after the oracle:

> Christ, then, was holy, and like the holy, went to the heaven. Wherefore you will say no evil about Him, but pity the folly of men." So says Porphyry even now. Was He then a charlatan, my friend? Perhaps the friendly words of one of your kidney may put you out of countenance. For you have our Saviour Jesus, the Christ of God, admitted by your own teachers

> to be, not an enchanter or a sorcerer, but holy, wise, the justest of the just, and dwelling in the vaults of heaven.
>
> (3.7)

Eusebius picks apart the ideas of Porphyry here and in his *Preparation for the Gospel* (Books 1; 3–6; 8–10; 11.27–28; 14.9–10), attempting to show that he was self-contradictory and could be refuted by other pagan authors who had written on oracles in the past such as Oenomaus the second-century Cynic (*Preparation for the Gospel* Book 5; 6.7) and Plutarch (*Preparation for the Gospel* Books 3 and 5; 11.10, 35–36; 14.13–16; 15.22–23 and 31–32) or Diogenianus, an Epicurean (*Preparation for the Gospel* 4.3; 6.7–8). Eusebius was able to draw on a rich tradition of both pagan and Christian writings that had grown up over time, particularly in the second century.

It is Lactantius in his *Divine Institutes* who explains how pagan oracles were involved in the persecution which began under Diocletian. Lactantius records that it was the practice of Christians, when present at a sacrifice, to banish the daemons who made it effective, by making the sign of the cross. When this practice was carried out at an imperial sacrifice, the pagan soothsayers, recognizing what was happening, informed the emperor, and this was the starting point of the Diocletian persecution.

> Diocletian, as being of a timorous disposition, was a searcher into futurity, and during his abode in the East he began to slay victims, that from their livers he might obtain a prognostic of events; and while he sacrificed, some attendants of his, who were Christians, stood by, and they put the immortal sign on their foreheads. At this the demons were chased away, and the holy rites interrupted. The soothsayers trembled, unable to investigate the wonted marks on the entrails of the victims. They frequently repeated the sacrifices, as if the former had been unpropitious; but the victims, slain from time to time, afforded no tokens for divination. At length Tages, the chief of the soothsayers, either from guess or from his own observation, said, There are profane persons here, who obstruct the rites. Then Diocletian, in furious passion, ordered not only all who were assisting at the holy ceremonies, but also all who resided within the palace, to sacrifice, and, in case of their refusal, to be scourged. And further, by letters to the commanding officers, he enjoined that all soldiers should be forced to the like impiety, under pain of being dismissed the service. Thus far his rage proceeded; but at that season he did nothing more against the law and religion of God. After an interval of some time he went to winter in Bithynia;

> and presently Galerius Caesar came there, inflamed with furious resentment, and purposing to excite the inconsiderate old man to carry on that persecution which he had begun against the Christians. I have learned that the cause of his fury was as follows.
>
> (*Of the Manner in which the Persecutors Died* 10; cp. *Divine Institutes* 4.27).

Later, before fully committing to the persecution, Diocletian sent to the oracle at Didyma for guidance as to whether he should proceed; he received a favorable answer: "He determined above all to consult his gods; and to that end he dispatched a soothsayer to inquire of Apollo at Miletus, whose answer was such as might be expected from an enemy of the divine religion" (11). Parke notes that a fragmentary inscription from the period of the Tetrarchy that mentions "the emperors," "Christians," and "the god" may possibly record an oracular response relating to this persecution (*Did.* II, 306).[67] And Eusebius' *Life of Constantine* 2.50 transcribes a letter of the emperor Constantine in which he blames Apollo for having incited the persecution.

The sources for the third century and the persecution under Diocletian indicate that both pagan individuals and emperors were looking to traditional religion to help them deal with the ever-growing numbers of Christians. They wanted to know what Apollo thought of the new religion. What did Apollo think of their god? The oracular responses indicate disdain and disapproval. Acrimonious discourse increased across the second and third centuries culminating in physical confrontation. Long-running arguments over prophecy and prophetic texts had come to a crossroads.

Notes

1 On incubation oracles, see Sarah Iles Johnston, *Ancient Greek Divination* (Malden, MA: Wiley-Blackwell, 2008); and Juliette Harrisson, *Dreams and Dreaming in the Roman Empire: Cultural Memory and Imagination* (New York: Bloomsbury, 2013), 233–36.

2 H.W. Parke, *The Oracles of Apollo in Asia Minor* (London: Croom Helm, 1985), 76–111.

3 Ibid., 160–62 and Eric Birley, "Cohors I Tungrorum and the Oracle of Clarion Apollo," *Chiron* 4 (1974): 511–13; for records of the delegations see Jean-Louis Ferrary, *Les mémoriaux de délégations du sanctuaire oraculaire de Claros, d'après la documentation conservée dans le fonds Louis Robert* (Paris: Académie des inscriptions et belles-lettres, 2014).

4 Parke, *Oracles of Apollo in Asia Minor*, 142–70.

5 The possible evidence is in *Greek Anthology* 11.161 and 163; see H.W. Parke, *Oracles of Apollo: Dodona, Olympia, Ammon* (Cambridge, MA: Harvard University Press, 1967), 189–90.
6 See Johnston, *Ancient Greek Divination* on Dodona; see Parke for the Roman imperial period, Parke, *Oracles of Apollo: Dodona, Olympia, Ammon*, 124–25.
7 See Parke, *Oracles of Apollo: Dodona, Olympia, Ammon*, 242.
8 See Lightfoot on this text and on divination by statues in antiquity, J.L. Lightfoot, ed., *Lucian, on the Syrian Goddess* (Oxford: Oxford University Press, 2003); on divination by statues in Egypt, see David Frankfurter, *Religion in Roman Egypt: Assimilation and Resistance* (Princeton, NJ: Princeton University Press, 1998), 145–97 and 233–51; for Egyptian oracles see Frankfurter, *Religion in Roman Egypt* and also his 2005 work, "Voices, Books, and Dreams: The Diversification of Divination Media in Late Antique Egypt," in *Mantikê: Studies in Ancient Divination*, eds. Sarah Iles Johnston and Peter Struck. Leiden: Brill, 2005.
9 Parke, *Oracles of Apollo*, 179–80.
10 Ibid., 176–77.
11 Ibid., 180–82.
12 Ibid., 188–93.
13 On this text see R. Bracht Branham, "The Comic as Critic: Revenging Epicurus: A Study of Lucian's Art of Comic Narrative," *Classical Antiquity* 3.2 (1984): 143–63.
14 For an overview of the evidence, see C.P. Jones, *Culture and Society in Lucian* (Cambridge, MA: Harvard University Press, 1986), 137–46.
15 See Hippolytus, *Refutation of all Heresies* 4.41 on the use of a crane's windpipes to make a skull speak. Richard Stoneman, *The Ancient Oracles: Making the Gods Speak* (New Haven, CT: Yale University Press, 2011), 67–69, connects this to divination by the dead.
16 Parke, *Oracles of Apollo in Asia Minor*, 194–96.
17 Ibid., 175.
18 Hans Dieter Betz, *The Greek Magical Papyri in Translation, Including the Demotic Spells: Volume 1* (Chicago: University of Chicago Press, 1986).
19 See David S. Potter, *Prophets and Emperors: Human and Divine Authority from Augustus to Theodosius* (Cambridge, MA: Harvard University Press, 1994), 31 for the papyrus evidence for this.
20 The technical term is Homeromanteion; see *PGM* 7.1–148. On the later dating of this (fourth-fifth century CE), see Andromache Karanika, "Homer the Prophet: Homeric Verses and Divination in the Homeromanteion," in *Sacred Words: Orality, Literacy, and Religion*, eds. A.P.M.H. Lardinois, J.H. Blok, and M.G.M. van der Poel (Leiden; Boston, MA: Brill, 2011), 255–78. *P. Oxy*. 56. 3831 dates to the third or fourth century CE. For Christian usage of the *Sortes Astrampsychi* and the oracle text, *Gospel of the Lots of Mary*, see AnneMarie Luijendijk, *Forbidden Oracles? The Gospel of the Lots of Mary* (Tübingen: Mohr Siebeck, 2014); for a general overview, see Richard Stoneman, *The Ancient Oracles: Making the Gods Speak* (New Haven, CT: Yale University Press, 2011), 144–48.
21 For more references see Mary Beard, John North, and Simon Price, *Religions of Rome: Volume 1: A History* (Cambridge: Cambridge University Press, 1998), 153 n. 108.

22 Potter, *Prophets and Emperors*, uses Latin epic as an illustrating example of the way that divination appeared in literature. We might also note that Naevius had written a play entitled, the *Soothsayer* (Aulus Gellius, *Attic Nights* 3.3) and Plautus' plays included soothsayers as characters or mentioned them (*Amphitryon, or Jupiter in Disguise* act 5; *Curculio, or The Forgery* act 4, scene 1; *Menaechmi, or The Twin Brothers* prologue act 5, scene 1; *Mercator, or The Merchant* act 5, scene 2; *Poenulus, or The Young Carthaginian* act 2, scene 1; *Rudens, or The Fisherman's Rope* act 2, scene 3; *Truculentus, or The Churl* act 2, scene 7; also Terence, *Phormio, or The Scheming Parasite* act 4, scene 4). For Theurgists who wrote about oracles in the third century, see Crystal Addey, *Divination and Theurgy in Neoplatonism: Oracles of the Gods* (Burlington, VT: Ashgate, 2014) and the end of this chapter.

23 Beard, North, and Price, *Religions of Rome*, 103; John Scheid, *An Introduction to Roman Religion* (Edinburgh: Edinburgh University Press, 2003), 143.

24 Scheid, *Introduction to Roman Religion*, 133.

25 Ibid., 134.

26 See Beard, North, and Price, *Religions of Rome*, 21–22 for more detail.

27 Scheid, *Introduction to Roman Religion*, 141.

28 Ibid., 130.

29 Ibid., 131.

30 See Beard, North, and Price, *Religions of Rome*, 21.

31 Ibid., 21–22; Scheid, *Introduction to Roman Religion*, 134.

32 Beard, North, and Price, *Religions of Rome*, 19–20 and 37.

33 Ibid., 20.

34 Ibid., 320, 326.

35 See H.W. Parke, *Sibyls and Sibylline Prophecy in Classical Antiquity* (London: Routledge, 1988), 215 n. 45 on these last two points.

36 For a discussion of the number of pagan oracles preserved and bibliography on this point, see Rieuwerd Buitenwerf, *Book Three of the Sibylline Oracles and Its Social Setting* (Boston, MA: Brill, 2003), 102 n. 36. A summary of the Secular Games and their relationship to the Books is found in a third-century author, Censorinus: "As to the Ages of Rome, some authors think they are (also) measured by the Cyclical Games or Ludi Saeculares." If this opinion is held to be true, the duration of the Roman cycles is vague, because both the interval of time at which the Games were formerly celebrated and even the epoch at which they should be held, is uncertain. Their return was fixed after each hundredth year. So thought Valerius Antias and other historians and also Varro, who, in his first book, *De Scenicis Originibus*, thus expresses himself:

> As numerous wonders were manifested and the wall and tower which are between the Colline and the Equiline Gates were struck by the fire of heaven, the decemvirs, after having interrogated the Sibylline books, declared that the Ludi Terentini must be celebrated in the Camp of Mars in honour of Pluto and Proserpine, and that black victims should be immolated to these gods, adding that the games should be renewed every one hundred years.

We read also in Titus Livius, book 136:11 "In the same year Divus Augustus revived with great pomp those Ludi Saeculares which it is customary to celebrate every hundred years, in other words, at the end of each cycle." On the contrary, if we refer either to the Commentaries of the Quindecemvirs, or to the edicts of the god Augustus (Divus Augustus) they should recur every one hundred years. Horace Flaccus, also, in the hymn which was sung at the Ludi Saeculares of his time, designated the epoch in the following terms: "A revolution of ten times eleven years brings back these games and hymns at which the people assemble during three days of splendour and as many nights of gladness." (Censorinus, *The Natal Day* 17.8; taken from *De Die Natale*, by Censorinus, translated into English by William Maude, New York: Cambridge Encyclopedia, 1900); see also Phlegon of Tralles, (second century CE) *Book of Marvels* and Tacitus, *Annals* 11.11.

37 See Potter, *Prophets and Emperors* for an in-depth analysis.

38 For Jews see Chapter 1; for Egyptians, see Potter, *Prophets and Emperors*, 171, 192–203; John J. Collins, *Seers, Sibyls & Sages in Hellenistic-Roman Judaism* (Leiden: E. J. Brill, 1997), 203–6; David Frankfurter, *Elijah in Upper Egypt: The Apocalypse of Elijah and Early Egyptian Christianity* (Minneapolis, MN: Fortress Press, 1993), 102, 161, 164–88; see 195–238 for Christian utilization of native Egyptian prophetic traditions in that apocalypse.

39 According to Beard, North, and Price, *Religions of Rome*, 231–33; Potter, *Prophets and Emperors*, 174–77; overall the bans were temporary or against certain pressing targets.

40 Potter, *Prophets and Emperors*, has the most complete record and analysis of these. The astrologer Scribonius predicted that the child Tiberius would rise to greatness (Suetonius, *Life of Tiberius* 14.4). Tiberius is said to have consulted astrologers regularly and to have retained one among his circle of intimates (Tacitus, *Annals* 6.20–21; Cassius Dio 58.27.1–3; Suetonius, *Life of Gaius* 19.3). Galba, like Otho and his astrologers, also was encouraged to revolt due to favorable signs and prognostications (Suetonius, *Life of Galba* 9). Titus visited the oracle of Aphrodite on Paphos (Tacitus, *Histories* 2.2–4). Cassius Dio provides a record of seven different signs that had encouraged Severus to seek the emperorship (75.3); for later sources and emperors, see Potter, *Prophets and Emperors*.

41 Clifford Ando, *Imperial Ideology and Provincial Loyalty in the Roman Empire* (Berkeley: University of California Press, 2000), part III: From *Imperium* to *Patria*.

42 See Parke, *Oracles of Apollo in Asia Minor*, chapter 5 for the epigraphic evidence.

43 For an overview of the Hermetic writings, see Brian P. Copenhauer, *Hermetica: The Greek Corpus Hermeticum and the Latin Asclepius in a New English Translation, with Notes and Introduction* (Cambridge: Cambridge University Press, 1992), xiii–lxi, or, more recently, Florian Ebeling, *The Secret History of Hermes Trismegistus: Hermeticism from Ancient to Modern Times*, trans. David Lorton (Ithaca, NY: Cornell University Press, 2007), 10–11.

44 From a Greek original, which was also translated in the Latin *Asclepius* mentioned earlier.

45 Addey, *Divination and Theurgy*, 8–9.

46 The *Chaldean Oracles* provided a paradigm of theurgic divination, ibid., 3, 8 and 25.
47 Ibid., 127–69.
48 Ibid., 239–41, for the hierarchy of divination.
49 See Ibid., 241, 249; see also Crystal Addey, "Oracles, "Dreams and Astrology in Iamblichus' *De mysteriis*," in *Seeing with Different Eyes: Essays in Astrology and Divination*, eds. Patrick Curry and Angela Voss (Cambridge: Cambridge Scholars, 2007), 35–57; Peter T. Struck, "Iamblichus on Divination: Divine Power and Human Intuition," in *Divine Powers in Late Antiquity*, eds. Anna Marmodoro and Irini-Fotini Viltanioti (Oxford: Oxford University Press, 2017), 75–87, especially 78–84); on comparison with Stoics, see Struck, "A World Full of Signs: Understanding Divination in Ancient Stoicism," in *Seeing with Different Eyes: Essays in Astrology and Divination*, eds. Patrick Curry and Angela Voss (Cambridge: Cambridge Scholars, 2007), 3–20.
50 Discussed in Addey, *Divination and Theurgy*, 264.
51 Ibid., 265–66.
52 Translation taken from Iamblichus, *On the Mysteries*, trans. Emma C. Clarke, John M. Dillon, and Jackson P. Hershbell (Atlanta: Society of Biblical Literature, 2003), 200–201.
53 Robert M. Berchman, *Porphyry against the Christians* (Leiden: Brill, 2005), 206.
54 Addey, *Divination and Theurgy*, 17–18.
55 Ibid., 154; Addey discusses Porphyry's connection to theurgy 9–10, 98–102, 127–69; see Struck, "Iamblichus on Divination," 78.
56 Addey, *Divination and Theurgy*, 98–106.
57 Ibid., 252–55.
58 For the sympathy principle, see Addey, *Divination and Theurgy*, 29–30; see Struck, "World Full of Signs," 7–9 for differences in the concept of sympathy in magical, medical, and Stoic texts.
59 All excerpts of this work are taken from Eusebius of Caesarea, *Praeparatio Evangelica*, trans. E.H. Gifford (Oxford: Typographeo Academico, 1903).
60 Berchman, *Porphyry*, 9.
61 Ibid., 58.
62 Ibid.
63 Translation is taken from *Jerome's Commentary on Daniel*, trans. Gleason Leonard Archer (Grand Rapids, MI: Baker Book House, 1958).
64

> This man, in truth, who overthrew his own arguments by his character, or censured his own character by his arguments, a weighty censor and most keen accuser against himself, at the very same time in which a righteous people were impiously assailed, vomited forth three books against the Christian religion and name; professing, above all things, that it was the office of a philosopher to remedy the errors of men, and to recall them to the true way, that is, to the worship of the gods, by whose power and majesty, as he said, the world is governed; and not to permit that inexperienced men should be enticed by the frauds of any, lest their simplicity should be a prey and sustenance to crafty men.
> (Lactantius, *Divine Institutes* 5.2)

It is impossible to say for certain, but it is plausible to think so; for a detailed argument on this point, see Elizabeth DePalma Digeser, “Lactantius, Porphyry, and the Debate over Religious Toleration,” *Journal of Roman Studies* 88 (1998): 129–46.

65 See also *Divine Institutes* 1.4, 6–7; 2. 9, 11, 16–17; 5.14; 6.25; 7.4, 7, 13, 15, 18–20, 23–25.

66 All translations of this text are taken from Eusebius of Caesarea, *Demonstratio Evangelica*, trans. W. J. Ferrar (London: S.P.C.K., 1920).

67 Parke, *Oracles of Apollo in Asia Minor*, 108.

Translations

Betz, Hans Dieter. *The Greek Magical Papyri in Translation, Including the Demotic Spells*. Volume 1. Chicago: University of Chicago Press, 1986.

Cicero. *On Old Age. On Friendship. On Divination.* Translated by W.A. Falconer. Loeb Classical Library 154. Cambridge, MA: Harvard University Press, 1923.

Dio Cassius. *Roman History, Volume VI: Books 51–55*. Translated by Earnest Cary and Herbert B. Foster. Loeb Classical Library 83. Cambridge, MA: Harvard University Press, 1917.

Dio Cassius. *Roman History, Volume VII: Books 56–60*. Translated by Earnest Cary and Herbert B. Foster. Loeb Classical Library 175. Cambridge, MA: Harvard University Press, 1924.

Dio Cassius. *Roman History, Volume VIII: Books 61–70*. Translated by Earnest Cary and Herbert B. Foster. Loeb Classical Library 176. Cambridge, MA: Harvard University Press, 1925.

Dionysius of Halicarnassus. *Roman Antiquities, Volume II: Books 3–4*. Translated by Earnest Cary. Loeb Classical Library 347. Cambridge, MA: Harvard University Press, 1939.

Eusebius of Caesarea. *Praeparatio Evangelica*. Translated by E. H. Gifford. Oxford: Typographeo Academico, 1903.

Eusebius of Caesarea. *Demonstratio Evangelica*. Translated by W. J. Ferrar. London: S.P.C.K., 1920.

Fathers of the Third Century: Tertullian, Part Fourth; Minucius Felix; Commodian; Origen, Part First and Second. Translated by Robert Ernest Wallis. Edited by Alexander Roberts and James Donaldson. Revised and chronologically arranged with brief prefaces and occasional notes by A. Cleveland Coxe. Ante-Nicene Fathers 4. New York: Christian Literature, 1885.

Fathers of the Third and Fourth Centuries: Lactantius, Venantius, Asterius, Victorinus, Dionysius, Apostolic Teaching and Constitutions, Homily, and Liturgy. Translated by William Fletcher. Edited by Alexander Roberts and James Donaldson. Revised and chronologically arranged with brief prefaces and occasional notes by A. Cleveland Coxe. Ante-Nicene Fathers 7. New York: Christian Literature, 1886.

Iamblichus. *On the Mysteries*. Translated by Emma C. Clarke, John M. Dillon, and Jackson P. Hershbell. Atlanta: Society of Biblical Literature, 2003.

Jerome's Commentary on Daniel. Translated by Gleason Leonard Archer. Grand Rapids, MI: Baker Book House, 1958.

Josephus. *The Jewish War, Volume III: Books 5–7*. Translated by H. St. J. Thackeray. Loeb Classical Library 210. Cambridge, MA: Harvard University Press, 1928.

Lucian. *Anacharsis or Athletics. Menippus or the Descent into Hades. On Funerals. A Professor of Public Speaking. Alexander the False Prophet. Essays in Portraiture. Essays in Portraiture Defended. The Goddesse of Surrye*. Translated by A.M. Harmon. Loeb Classical Library 162. Cambridge, MA: Harvard University Press, 1925.

Pausanias. *Description of Greece, Volume I: Books 1–2 (Attica and Corinth)*. Translated by W.H.S. Jones. Loeb Classical Library 93. Cambridge, MA: Harvard University Press, 1918.

Pausanias. *Description of Greece, Volume III: Books 6–8.21 (Elis 2, Achaia, Arcadia)*. Translated by W.H.S. Jones. Loeb Classical Library 272. Cambridge, MA: Harvard University Press, 1933.

Plutarch. *Moralia, Volume VII: On Love of Wealth. On Compliancy. On Envy and Hate. On Praising Oneself Inoffensively. On the Delays of the Divine Vengeance. On Fate. On the Sign of Socrates. On Exile. Consolation to His Wife*. Translated by Phillip H. De Lacy and Benedict Einarson. Loeb Classical Library 405. Cambridge, MA: Harvard University Press, 1959.

St. Augustin's City of God and Christian Doctrine. Edited by Philip Schaff. A Select Library of the Nicene and Post-Nicene Fathers of the Christian Church 2. Buffalo: Christian Literature, 1887.

Suetonius. *Lives of the Caesars, Volume I: Julius. Augustus. Tiberius. Gaius. Caligula*. Translated by J.C. Rolfe. Introduction by K.R. Bradley. Loeb Classical Library 31. Cambridge, MA: Harvard University Press, 1914.

Strabo. *Geography, Volume III: Books 6–7*. Translated by Horace Leonard Jones. Loeb Classical Library 182. Cambridge, MA: Harvard University Press, 1924.

Strabo. *Geography, Volume VI: Books 13–14*. Translated by Horace Leonard Jones. Loeb Classical Library 223. Cambridge, MA: Harvard University Press, 1929.

Strabo. *Geography, Volume VIII: Book 17. General Index*. Translated by Horace Leonard Jones. Loeb Classical Library 267. Cambridge, MA: Harvard University Press, 1932.

Tacitus. *Annals: Books 4–6, 11–12*. Translated by John Jackson. Loeb Classical Library 312. Cambridge, MA: Harvard University Press, 1937.

Valerius Maximus. *Memorable Doings and Sayings, Volume I: Books 1–5*. Edited and translated by D.R. Shackleton Bailey. Loeb Classical Library 492. Cambridge, MA: Harvard University Press, 2000.

Bibliography

Addey, Crystal. *Divination and Theurgy in Neoplatonism: Oracles of the Gods*. Burlington, VT: Ashgate, 2014.

———. "Oracles, 'Dreams and Astrology in Iamblichus' *De mysteriis*." In *Seeing with Different Eyes: Essays in Astrology and Divination*, edited by Patrick Curry and Angela Voss, 35–57. Cambridge Scholars, 2007.

Ando, Clifford. *Imperial Ideology and Provincial Loyalty in the Roman Empire*. Berkeley: University of California Press, 2000.

Beard, Mary, John North, and Simon Price. *Religions of Rome: Volume 1: A History*. Cambridge: Cambridge University Press, 1998.

Berchman, Robert M. *Porphyry against the Christians*. Leiden: Brill, 2005.

Birley, Eric. "Cohors I Tungrorum and the Oracle of Clarion Apollo." *Chiron* 4 (1974): 511–13.

Branham, Bracht R. "The Comic as Critic: Revenging Epicurus: A Study of Lucian's Art of Comic Narrative." *Classical Antiquity* 3.2 (1984): 143–63.

Buitenwerf, Rieuwerd. *Book Three of the Sibylline Oracles and Its Social Setting*. Boston, MA: Brill, 2003.

Collins, John J. *Seers, Sibyls & Sages in Hellenistic-Roman Judaism*. Leiden: E.J. Brill, 1997.

Copenhauer, Brian P. *Hermetica: The Greek Corpus Hermeticum and the Latin Asclepius in a New English Translation, with Notes and Introduction*. Cambridge: Cambridge University Press, 1992.

DePalma Digeser, Elizabeth. "Lactantius, Porphyry, and the Debate over Religious Toleration." *Journal of Roman Studies* 88 (1998): 129–46.

Ebeling, Florian. *The Secret History of Hermes Trismegistus: Hermeticism from Ancient to Modern Times*. Translated by David Lorton. Ithaca, NY: Cornell University Press.

Ferrary, Jean-Louis. *Les mémoriaux de délégations du sanctuaire oraculaire de Claros, d'après la documentation conservée dans le fonds Louis Robert*. Paris: Académie des inscriptions et belles-lettres, 2014.

Frankfurter, David. *Elijah in Upper Egypt: The Apocalypse of Elijah and Early Egyptian Christianity*. Minneapolis, MN: Fortress Press, 1993.

———. *Religion in Roman Egypt: Assimilation and Resistance*. Princeton, NJ: Princeton University Press, 1998.

———. "Voices, Books, and Dreams: The Diversification of Divination Media in Late Antique Egypt." In *Mantikê: Studies in Ancient Divination*, edited by Sarah Iles Johnston and Peter Struck, 233–54. Leiden: Brill, 2005.

Johnston, Sarah Iles. *Ancient Greek Divination*. Malden, MA: Wiley-Blackwell, 2008.

Jones, C.P. *Culture and Society in Lucian*. Cambridge, MA: Harvard University Press, 1986.

Karanika, Andromache. "Homer the Prophet: Homeric Verses and Divination in the Homeromanteion." In *Sacred Words: Orality, Literacy, and Religion*, edited by A.P.M.H. Lardinois, J.H. Blok, and M.G.M. van der Poel, 255–78. Leiden; Boston, MA: Brill, 2011.

Lightfoot, J.L., ed. *Lucian: On the Syrian Goddess*. Oxford: Oxford University Press, 2003.

Luijendijk, AnneMarie. *Forbidden Oracles? The Gospel of the Lots of Mary*. Tübingen: Mohr Siebeck, 2014.

Parke, H.W. *The Oracles of Apollo: Dodona, Olympia, Ammon*. Cambridge, MA: Harvard University Press, 1967.

———. *The Oracles of Apollo in Asia Minor*. London: Croom Helm, 1985.

———. *Sibyls and Sibylline Prophecy in Classical Antiquity*. London: Routledge, 1988.

Potter, David S. *Prophets and Emperors: Human and Divine Authority from Augustus to Theodosius*. Cambridge, MA: Harvard University Press, 1994.

Scheid, John. *An Introduction to Roman Religion*. Originally published in French as *La Religion des Romains*. Paris, 1998. Translated by Janet Lloyd. Edinburgh: Edinburgh University Press, 2003.

Stoneman, Richard. *The Ancient Oracles: Making the Gods Speak*. New Haven, CT: Yale University Press, 2011.

Struck, Peter T. "Iamblichus on Divination: Divine Power and Human Intuition." In *Divine Powers in Late Antiquity*, edited by Anna Marmodoro and Irini-Fotini Viltanioti, 75–87. Oxford: Oxford University Press, 2017.

———. "A World Full of Signs: Understanding Divination in Ancient Stoicism." In *Seeing with Different Eyes: Essays in Astrology and Divination*, edited by Patrick Curry and Angela Voss, 3–20. Cambridge: Cambridge Scholars, 2007.

Conclusion

> Greeks and Barbarians alike testify to the existence of oracles and oracular responses in all parts of the earth, and they say that they were revealed by the foresight of the Creator for the use and profit of men, so that there need be no essential difference between Hebrew prophecy and the oracles of the other nations. For as the Supreme God gave oracles to the Hebrews through their prophets, and suggested what was to their advantage, so also He gave them to the other nations through their local oracles. For He was not only the God of the Jews, but of the rest of mankind as well; and He cared not more for these than those, but His Providence was over all alike, just as He has given the sun ungrudgingly for all, and not for the Hebrews only, and the supply of needs according to the seasons, and a like bodily constitution for all, and one mode of birth, and one kind of rational soul. And, thus, they say he provided ungrudgingly for all men the science of foretelling the future, to some by prophets, to some by oracles, to some by the flight of birds, or by inspecting entrails, or by dreams, or omens contained in word or sound, or by some other sign. For these they say were bestowed on all men by the Providence of God, so that the prophets of the Hebrews should not seem to have an advantage over the rest of the world.
>
> (Eusebius, *Demonstration of the Gospel* 5, pref.)[1]

In the Roman Empire, divination was accepted and practiced by Jews, Christians, and Greco-Roman pagans. Second Temple Judaism experienced prophecy through a received canon of texts, through the production of new prophetic texts, and through active, vocal, prophets. They used prophets and prophecy to help them make sense of their world, in particular in times of stress, to help them identify enemies, and to reach out to their pagan neighbors.

Christians had much work to do to establish and maintain their identity in the early centuries of the Empire, and they found prophecy and prophetic texts to be natural and useful tools in the effort to set themselves apart from Jews, heretics, and pagans. Irenaeus said that it was harder for Christians to convert pagans than it was for them to convert Jews because Christians and pagans did not share a common canon of prophetic texts. But Christians did utilize the pagan belief in prophecy (the proof of prophecy!), as a method of conversion, and they adapted the Jewish strategy of appropriating a common oracular figure, the Sibyl.

Divination was a part of the state apparatus of the Roman Empire. Greeks and Romans consulted oracles for guidance in their daily lives and also considered them to be a sure source of knowledge about religion (the will and nature of the gods; proper religious rites). Neoplatonists and theurgists analyzed oracular responses and sought to unite fully with the divine through purification and divination. Pagans of the Roman imperial period criticized Christian methods of interpretation with respect to prophetic texts, and they also accused them of creating false oracles (such as the Christianized *Sibylline Oracles*). In the face of a growing Christian Church they turned to their oracles for answers about this new religion. Anti-Christian polemic about prophets, prophecy, and oracles fed into persecution.

But Christians survived the period of persecution, and we see a triumphant Christian attitude quite clearly in the third- and fourth-century Christian responses to Porphyry. In Eusebius' works, Jewish prophetic texts have become Christian prophetic texts, and the daemonic forces responsible for pagan oracles cannot help but testify to the truth of the Christian faith before succumbing at last to utter defeat and disappearing forever.

This book has surveyed the uses and function of prophecy, prophets, and oracles among Jews, Christians, and pagans in the first three centuries of the Roman Empire and explored how prophecy and prophetic texts functioned as a common language that enabled religious discourse to develop between these groups. This work has shown that each of these cultures believed that it was in prophetic texts and prophetic utterances that they could find the surest proof of their beliefs and a strong confirmation of their group identity. Jews, Christians, and pagans attached great weight to prophecy. It is difficult to imagine what their religious systems would look like without it. All three saw prophetic signs and texts as the means of salvation and a sure sign of Divine Providence.

Note

1 Translation taken from Eusebius of Caesarea, *Demonstratio Evangelica*, trans. W. J. Ferrar (London: S.P.C.K., 1920).

Translation

Eusebius of Caesarea. *Demonstratio Evangelica*. Translated by W. J. Ferrar. London: S.P.C.K., 1920.

Index

Page numbers followed by n indicate notes.

Helping you to choose the right eBooks for your Library

Add Routledge titles to your library's digital collection today. Taylor and Francis ebooks contains over 50,000 titles in the Humanities, Social Sciences, Behavioural Sciences, Built Environment and Law.

Choose from a range of subject packages or create your own!

Benefits for you

- Free MARC records
- COUNTER-compliant usage statistics
- Flexible purchase and pricing options
- All titles DRM-free.

REQUEST YOUR FREE INSTITUTIONAL TRIAL TODAY

Free Trials Available
We offer free trials to qualifying academic, corporate and government customers.

Benefits for your user

- Off-site, anytime access via Athens or referring URL
- Print or copy pages or chapters
- Full content search
- Bookmark, highlight and annotate text
- Access to thousands of pages of quality research at the click of a button.

eCollections – Choose from over 30 subject eCollections, including:

- Archaeology
- Architecture
- Asian Studies
- Business & Management
- Classical Studies
- Construction
- Creative & Media Arts
- Criminology & Criminal Justice
- Economics
- Education
- Energy
- Engineering
- English Language & Linguistics
- Environment & Sustainability
- Geography
- Health Studies
- History
- Language Learning
- Law
- Literature
- Media & Communication
- Middle East Studies
- Music
- Philosophy
- Planning
- Politics
- Psychology & Mental Health
- Religion
- Security
- Social Work
- Sociology
- Sport
- Theatre & Performance
- Tourism, Hospitality & Events

For more information, pricing enquiries or to order a free trial, please contact your local sales team: **www.tandfebooks.com/page/sales**

The home of Routledge books

www.tandfebooks.com

www.ingramcontent.com/pod-product-compliance
Ingram Content Group UK Ltd.
Pitfield, Milton Keynes, MK11 3LW, UK
UKHW020347010325
455677UK00021B/333